D1399622

Hans-Ruedi Weber / Jesus and the Children

Hans-Ruedi Weber

Jesus and the Children

Biblical Resources for Study and Preaching

John Knox Press
ATLANTA

Unless specified otherwise, *Bible quotations* are taken from the Revised Standard Version by permission of the Division of Christian Education of the NCCC/USA.

All texts from ancient *Greek and Latin authors* (including Josephus) are quoted according to the translations published in Loeb Classical Library by permission of Harvard University Press, William Heinemann.

With a few exceptions, the various *rabbinic sayings* are quoted either from the translations in H. Danby: *The Mishnah* (for texts from the *Mishnah*, by permission of Oxford University Press) and from C. C. Montefiori and H. Loewe: *A Rabbinic Anthology* (for texts from Babylonian and Jerusalem *Talmud*, *Tosefta*, etc., by permission of The Jewish Publication Society of America, Philadelphia). A few texts not found in the above two volumes have been translated from German quotations in H. L. Strack — P. Billerbeck: *Kommentar zum Neuen Testament aus Talmud und Midrasch*, München, 1961.

The *Targum* on Exodus 15 : 2 is taken from P. Winter: "Lc 2, 49 and Talmud Yerushalmi" in *Zeitschrift für die neutestamentliche Wissenschaft* 45, 1954, pp. 145-179, and the English translation of *Soferim* 18 : 5 is quoted from J. Jeremias: *Infant Baptism in the First Four Centuries*, London, 1960, p. 49, by permission of SCM Press, London.

Quotations from the Gospel of Thomas are taken from E. Hennecke: *New Testament Apocrypha*, Vol. I, by permission of Lutterworth Press, London. "Justin's First Apology" is quoted from A. Roberts and J. Donaldson (eds): *The Ante-Nicene Fathers*, Vol. I, p. 172, by permission of Wm. B. Eerdmans Publishing Co., Grand Rapids.

Library of Congress Cataloging in Publication Data

Weber, Hans Ruedi.
    Jesus and the children.

    Bibliography: p.
      1. Jesus Christ—Attitude toward children.
I. Title.
BT590.C48W4   239.9′5   79-87754
ISBN 0-8042-1316-X

First printed in Lausanne, Switzerland
© copyright 1979 by the World Council of Churches, Geneva
Printed in the United States of America by
John Knox Press
Atlanta, Georgia 1979

Contents

Introduction

1979: the International Year of the Child. Will adults look back sentimentally to their childhood and glamorize children as a new idol? Will 1979 see the beginning of new campaigns against infant mortality and the beating of children, and for better nutrition, and educational opportunities? Campaigns like these are necessary, and Christians must help to initiate and support them. But a great opportunity would be missed if this Year of the Child were to become just an occasion for sentimental festivities or good works which adults do *for* children, because a more sensitive life *together with* children can become for adults the source of deep insight into the secrets of life and an opportunity for spiritual growth.

What can we learn from Jesus' attitude to children for our common life with them and for our adult Christian life in the world? The study of some texts from the gospels is proposed here as an introduction to a discussion of this question. The following remarks will, hopefully, avoid false expectations and facilitate both the reading of this book and its use for study purposes.

There are only a *few biblical texts on Jesus and children*. It is true that the Bible contains many passages where the word "child", its synonyms and derivatives occur: the "children of Israel", "sons of Abraham", "daughters of Sion", "God's children", "my little children", and so on. However, all these expressions refer to a relationship or specify the origin of a person. They may include actual boys and girls, but they do not designate children as distinguished from adults. The biblical languages have different words for these different shades of meaning. In Appendix A, the use of these various terms in the New Testament will be briefly analysed.

The studies proposed do not concern such subjects as the titles, "Son of God" or "Son of Man", which are given to Jesus in the gospels. Nor are God's adoption of a people or the call to be God's children examined, though undoubtedly they are central themes in the Old Testament and are prominent in the letters of the New Testament. Also, the subject of the relationship between parents and children in the light of Jesus' proclamation of the Kingdom has been left out.

The texts proposed for study are only those where Jesus meets actual children. Chapter one deals with the parable of the children playing in the market place (Matt. 11 : 16-19 and Luke-7 : 31-35). Chapter two explores the story which lies behind the passage of Mark 10 : 13-16, in which children are brought to Jesus, and its parallels. In chapter three, a single saying of Jesus is examined which appears in different contexts and with different wording. It has to do with our calling to be like children (Mark 10 : 15, Luke 18 : 17 and Matt. 18 : 3). Finally, chapter four is devoted to the scene where Jesus puts a child in the midst of his disciples in order to teach them a lesson (Mark 9 : 33-37, Luke 9 : 46-48 and Matt. 18 : 1-5).

One might have added the story where Jesus brings back to life the twelve-year old daughter of Jairus (Mark 5 : 21 ff.). Yet this and similar passages where actual children are involved do not differ essentially from other gospel narratives of miracles and healings. More important for the particular subject of this study would be an examination of the texts on the children shouting "Hosanna to the Son of David" in the Temple (Matt. 21 : 15) and on the "babes" to whom the Good News has been revealed (Matt. 11 : 25-30 and Luke 10 : 21-22). It would also be interesting to include the passages about Jesus' own childhood (Luke 2 and Matt. 2) in such a study. This is more or less a complete, yet short, list of relevant texts about Jesus and the children. The four passages chosen are certainly the central ones.

Contrary to what one might expect, *the texts on Jesus and the children are difficult to understand.* A superficial reading of these passages can, of course, quickly lead to some general observations about the subject. Yet one risks to be deaf and blind to the particular nuances which Mark, Matthew and Luke each attempted to transmit and interpret concerning what happened when Jesus was in the company of children. Moreover, a superficial reading will not reveal that the very heart of the Christian Gospel is expressed in Jesus' gestures and sayings in relation to children.

There is no doubt that, behind the passages to be studied, lies the memory of events which happened in the earthly life of Jesus, of the gestures He made and the words He spoke. Neither is there any doubt that the reports we find now in the gospels are already varying interpretations of what Jesus did and said. In order to take this manifold biblical testimony seriously and, if possible, to penetrate from there to the actual events and sayings, it is necessary to compare the parallel accounts of the evangelists and to study each version in its own particular context. On the four worksheets in Appendix D, these testimonies are printed synoptically, that is, in parallel columns. The worksheets also indicate the varied contexts, and list some other biblical and extra-biblical texts for comparison. Readers are advised to tear out the worksheets. They can thus have the synoptically arranged testimonies of the evangelists before them while reading the interpretations proposed in this book. Even when the apostle Paul preached the Word of God, the mature congregation in Beroe'a was "examining the Scriptures daily to see if these things were so" (Acts 17 : 11). How much more should readers of this book check and double check on the basis of the evangelists' testimony to see whether it is really so!

I do not claim to have fully understood and explained the difficult texts about Jesus and the children. Readers who want to explore this subject in greater depth will find in Appendix B some bibliographical information which will help them further.

Jesus did not live in a vacuum. He was rooted in his environment and, at the same time, remarkably transcended his milieu. In order to explore this, special attention has been given to *the position of the child in the Graeco-Roman and Jewish world*. Instead of simply indicating where relevant passages can be found in the writings of Greek and Latin authors and in the labyrinth of rabbinic writings, I have quoted such passages extensively, because they would not otherwise be easily available for most readers. Some passages, which are too long to be fully quoted in the text, have been grouped together in Appendix C which serves as a small compendium on the child in the milieu of the New Testament.

Most of the Greek and Latin authors quoted wrote in the centuries immediately before and after Christ. The matter is more complicated with regard to sayings and stories of Jewish rabbis. Theirs was essentially an oral tradition, carefully memorized and transmitted from teacher to pupil. Towards 200 A.D., the main body of this oral tradition was finally set down in writing in the 39 tracts of the *Mishnah* (literally: "repetition") under rabbi Judah the Prince. This now codified tradition was again commented upon and expanded by the rabbis.

Later, the *Mishnah* together with the *Gemara* ("completion"), that is, the afore-mentioned additional comments, were again fixed in writing in the *Talmud* ("study"). The Jerusalem version of it was completed by 425 A.D., and the larger Babylonian *Talmud* only by 500 A.D. Besides these major codifications, other oral traditions were put down in writing such as the *Targum* (Aramaic paraphrase of biblical texts), the *Midrash* (narrative or legal "explanation" of biblical texts), the earliest Jewish prayer books and the *Tosefta* ("additions" to the *Mishnah*).

Unless otherwise specified, the rabbinic quotations in this book are taken from the Babylonian *Talmud*. While the authorities quoted in these sayings and stories may be rabbis living in the 2nd, 3rd or 4th centuries A.D., the thoughts expressed and information given are usually more ancient. Due to the oral tradition, some of them go back to pre-Christian times. Many of them (but it is, alas, uncertain which ones!) can give us an idea of what Jewish rabbis thought in the time of Jesus.

Many *important questions about Jesus and the children are not answered* in this book. Why is it that, when Jesus meets with children, He ends up by addressing his disciples, warning and teaching them? It cannot be emphasized too strongly that the passages proposed for study are not, in the first place, stories to be told to children in Sunday schools. Rather, they are radical challenges to adult Christians. Yet it would also be wrong to interpret the children in these passages exclusively as metaphors. Jesus *did* have a special relationship with actual children. What does this relationship teach us concretely for our adult Christian existence in the present world with all the important personal and social-ethical decisions to be made? In modern church life, a dangerous dichotomy can be observed. There are some churches whose life and worship is one-sidedly "children-centred", and other churches and Christian action groups who are so deeply involved in the big issues of our time that they forget the children and what Jesus teaches us through them. How can we avoid this dichotomy?

These questions cannot be discussed seriously unless one first listens carefully to the biblical testimony about Jesus and the children. The study outlines and worksheets in Appendix D may help groups to do this. Yet Bible study is not enough. Therefore, the study outlines also include some suggestions as to how study groups might proceed from Bible study to worship and action.

H.-R. W.

1 · We Piped to You and You Did Not Dance

Matthew 11:16-19; Luke 7:31-35

Play a joyous melody with a good rhythm and children will dance — certainly in Latin America or Africa. And so it should be, we think. But everybody who has lived with children knows that children do not always respond according to expectation. They sometimes sulk; often they spoil the game, either because they simply refuse to enter into it, or because they misunderstand the rules.

A children's game

Jesus must have often observed children at play. It may have reminded him of the time when He himself was a boy and played with other children of Nazareth in the market place. Here is a concrete case: a group of children sat and shouted at one another after a game which failed. Probably they had intended to play "marriage feast" and "burial". One group imitated the musicians at a marriage feast, but the others would not dance. Then they copied what adults do when someone dies and the body is prepared for burial, and the others failed to join in by mourning and weeping.

Neither Matthew's nor Luke's account of this incident indicates that the children were angry with one another. Possibly one group merely refused to join the game and was accused of lack of sportsmanship. It is more likely that the game consisted of a mime played by some of the children while others had to guess what the actions meant. And perhaps they guessed wrong and the actors shouted teasingly: "Wrong! You haven't understood it at all!" The words actually called out have rhythm and rhyme, as is often the case when children shout together. The boys and girls may, in fact, have taken up a familiar proverbial chorus to tease one another.

The evangelists testify on many occasions that it was everyday happenings of this kind in the villages and the countryside of Palestine which were revealing to Jesus. Like other Jewish rabbis, He used them as parables. Sometimes, such parables simply served as illustrations in teaching. On other occasions, Jesus discerned in everyday events deeply significant metaphors and parables of the Kingdom. In the case of the children's game in the market place, the parable played yet another role, namely, that of making a point vividly in the polemic debate with the Jewish crowd.

This polemic parable with its application became known to the evangelists through the oral tradition of the Church. It must have formed part of a collection of sayings of Jesus which Mark apparently did not know, but which was used by both Matthew and Luke. The parable was probably already among the special sayings related to events and pronouncements about John the Baptist. Matthew and Luke have considerably edited this traditional context according to their own particular understanding of Jesus. The parable itself and its application are narrated by both evangelists in almost the same manner. In the New Testament, most parables are told without an explicit application. The evangelists add one sentence at the most to the beginning or at the end to help readers get the point. In the case of the parable of the children's game, however, the application is as long as the text of the parable itself. This has misled many interpreters to explain the story on the basis of its application and to read into the simple parable things which are not, in fact, there.

Some have even made an allegory out of this story by assigning a special meaning to every detail and each actor. According to such an interpretation, the first group of children represent Jesus who came with an invitation to the messianic marriage feast. The second group is compared to John the Baptist who had earlier come with a call to conversion and contrition. Yet "this generation" misunderstands and rejects them both. This explanation of the parable does not do justice to a text where no identification of John and Jesus with the children is made. On the contrary, it is "this generation" which is like children. The comparison to be made between the parable story and human reality does not concern individual actors and incidents, but the whole astonishing course of events and its typical reversals. The children and their game which failed represent what happens when John (the predecessor of the Messiah) and the Messiah himself appear on the scene.

At this decisive hour of the history of salvation, one would expect sincere conversion and a deep joy. In a vision of the coming messianic age, the prophet Zechariah saw God not only "jealous for Zion with great wrath" (Zech 8 : 2), but also as the one who returns to the holy mountain and brings the remnant of his people there to live in peace: "Old men and old women shall again sit in the streets of Jerusalem, each with staff in hand for very age. And the streets of the city shall be full of boys and girls playing in its streets" (8 : 4 ff.). Such deep contentment one would expect. However, the children have spoiled or misunderstood the game. This whole incident is like "this generation" which has not understood John the Baptist, but calls him a madman (cf. John 7 : 20; 8 : 48, 52, where Jesus is considered to be mad). The whole incident shows the utter incomprehension of Jesus' contemporaries who mock the Messiah: "Behold, a glutton and a drunkard, a friend of tax collectors and sinners!"

Luke's and Matthew's version

The passage about the children's game is edited somewhat differently in Luke's and Matthew's gospel, both with regard to its context and its special emphasis (cf. Worksheet I in Appendix D). Even in the story of the parable and its application, some minor differences occur. According to Matthew, the children call "to the others", without specifying whether these were a group of other children or simply passers-by. Luke, however, clearly implies that two groups of children call "to one another". Nor does he write generally about any kind of "children sitting in the market places" of cities and villages, as Matthew does, but about a particular case, namely, these "children who are sitting in the market place". Furthermore, Luke writes about "weeping" while Matthew's version has "mourning". In the application of the parable, Luke specifies that in his ascetic life the Baptist ate "no bread" and drank "no wine". According to him, Jesus addressed thereby the hearers directly ("you say"), while Matthew uses the more general expression "they say". Far more important are the differences in the context of the whole passage and in the last sentence of the application. After the reversal of the unexpected response in the parable itself, both evangelists write about a second reversal in the concluding sentence.

According to Luke, Jesus said: "Yet wisdom is justified by all her children" (Luke 7 : 35). In verses 32 and 35, two different Greek words are used for designating the children. In the former, it is *paidion*, which means a child in contrast to an adult. In the latter verse, the term *teknon* is used, which refers to the origin, the link of paternity (cf. Appendix A). In the Old Testament and the intertestamental literature, the sages or wisdom personified frequently call those who follow their counsel "my son" or "my child" (Prov. 1 : 8, 10, 15; *Sirach* 2 : 1; 3 : 1). Similarly, wisdom is related here to "her children". It would therefore be wrong to equate "the children of wisdom" with the children of the parable.

Shocking as it may have sounded to Pharisees and lawyers who had studied the whole wisdom literature, the "children of wisdom" are here identified with "all the people and the tax collectors" who had been baptized by John. They were the ones who "justified God" (Luke 7 : 29 ff.).Luke singles out one of them in the passage immediately following: the woman who had sinned and who had come to anoint the feet of Jesus (vv. 36-50).

True wisdom is the "purpose of God" which becomes manifest in John's baptism (v. 30) and in the whole ministry of Jesus (vv. 21-23), and which is accepted by those who are ill, the poor, the outcasts and sinners. The "wise" Pharisees and the lawyers have rejected this purpose of God (v. 30) and "this generation" scoffs at Jesus because He is a friend of tax collectors and sinners. Yet those who acknowledge this strange wisdom of God to be just are now justified. *They* are the children of wisdom. The parable of the children in the market place serves, therefore, in Luke's gospel as the sombre background for the good news to tax collectors and sinners.

In Matthew's version, the accent lies more on the judgment over "this generation". The woes immediately following, poured on the cities of the northern shore of Lake Galilee emphasize this. The forerunner of the Messiah, Elijah, had come in the person of John the Baptist, and the Kingdom of Heaven was at hand (Matt. 11 : 12-15). The "deeds of the Christ" (v. 2), his healings and miracles, had been performed in those cities before the eyes of this very generation. Blessing falls on all who take no offence at such a Messiah (vv. 5-6). Yet this generation does take offence. It has no ears to hear (v. 15). Like the children of the parable it does not understand, misjudging both the Baptist and the Son of Man. In the second reversal of this situation, the "children of wisdom" do not appear in Matthew's account. Wisdom is justified "by her deeds" (v. 19c). This version — possibly an editorial change by Matthew — refers back to "the deeds of the Christ" in verse 2. Here, Christ and God's wisdom are almost identified with one another, and Christ's ministry vindicates the justice of God's wisdom. This justice means, first of all, judgment upon those who were supposed to recognize "the mighty works" of the Christ (v. 21). It also leads to thanksgiving for the gracious will of the Father, who has "hidden these things from the wise and understanding and revealed them to babes" (v. 25). The Greek term used here is *nēpios* (cf. Appendix A).

According to the accounts of both evangelists, Jesus saw in these particular children and their unsuccessful game a parable for "this generation". In the gospels, this expression is often used in a similarly pejorative way and it is current in the book of Deuteronomy. There, this expression designates the people of Israel during the exodus (Deut. 1 : 35; 32 : 5, 20). It is an "adulterous and sinful generation" (Mark 8 : 38; cf. Matt. 12 : 39; 16 : 4), a "faithless and perverse generation" (Matt. 17 : 17; Luke 9 : 41), which seeks signs and rejects the Son of Man (Luke 17 : 25). Like the writers of Deuteronomy and like the prophet Jeremiah (Jer. 7 : 29), Jesus addressed this strong language to his own people. In Matthew's gospel, "this generation" designates the Jews and especially their representative leaders in that decisive hour, when they were confronted with the proclamation of God's imminent Kingdom, but rejected the message. According to the context of Luke's version, "this generation" consists first of all of the Pharisees and lawyers (cf. Luke 7 : 30, 39). Yet it probably also has a wider reference to the whole of humanity as it faces God's purpose in Jesus Christ and does not recognize it. These Jews and gentiles are characterized by the children of the parable.

There is no romanticism in Jesus' evaluation of children. Sometimes they are touching in their spontaneous joy and expectancy. Often they astonish us with deep insights. Yet sometimes children sulk, and refuse to respond or understand. Jesus has closely observed them and in this particular parable the children and their game serve as a mirror of "this generation". This is not all that Jesus had to say about children. However, in the light of how children were seen in the Graeco-Roman and the Jewish world, it is important to notice first of all Jesus' realistic view of what children at play sometimes do.

The child among Greeks and Romans

In the Graeco-Roman world, children were generally held in very low esteem. Of course, procreation was necessary for the continuation of families and nations. Healthy sons, especially, were valued as future labourers and soldiers. But children had no worth in themselves, and their personality was seldom noticed. The Romans simply gave numbers to their daughters, and their sons were also given no names from the third or the fifth son onwards. For a long time, children appeared in Graeco-Roman art simply as small adults. Thus, childhood was seen as a weak, insignificant, biographical stage, a preface to adulthood.

The clearest manifestation of this low status was the widespread custom of casting out new-born infants. Children were in a literal sense disposable. A letter written in the year 1 B.C. by the Egyptian migrant labourer, Hilarion, to his pregnant wife, Alis, at home expresses this in an abrupt way: "Know that we are still in Alexandria... I beg and entreat you, take care of the little one, and as soon as we receive our pay I will send it up to you. If by chance you bear a child, if it is a boy, let it be; if it is a girl, cast it out..." (*Papyrus Oxyrhynchus* 744). The casting out of children, especially girls, the crippled and sickly, was common practice. The Greek historian, Plutarch, who wrote around 100 A.D., describes what happened in ancient Sparta when a child was born: "Offspring was not reared at the will of the father, but was taken and carried by him to a place called Lesche, where the elders of the tribes officially examined the infant, and if it was well-built and sturdy, they ordered the father to rear it, and assigned it one of the nine thousand lots of land; but if it was ill-born and deformed, they sent it to the so-called Apothetae, a chasm-like place at the foot of Mount Taÿgetus, in the conviction that the life of that which nature had not well equipped at the very beginning for health and strength was of no advantage either to itself or the state" (*Lycurgus* 16.1 ff.). In Rome, the new-born child was placed before its father's feet. Unless the father lifted it up and thus acknowledged the child, it was exposed. The Latin verb "to lift up" (*suscipere*) thus became a synonym for survival. Many of the exposed children died. Others were reared to become slaves. Boys might be forced to become gladiators while girls became prostitutes. The elder Seneca, a contemporary of Jesus, reports that in his time professional beggars would collect exposed children, mutilate them and use their misery for begging.

Child exposure may partly have been dictated by cultic motives. More often, it resulted from sheer poverty. Stobaeus, who in the 5th century A.D. collected ethical sayings of ancient Greek authors, includes the following laconic saying: "The poor man raises his sons, but daughters, if one is poor, we expose" (*Eclogae* 75). Rich parents also followed this custom. This can only be explained by the low esteem in which children, considered to be insignificant and disposable, were held. Such child exposure, coupled with prevention of pregnancy and abortion, led to depopulation. It is true that the stoic philosopher, Musonius, exalted parenthood and fought against the depreciation of women and children in the 1st century A.D. Even before him, Epictetus had protested against child exposure. However, the poetry of Ovid had more influence than such lonely voices. In this poetry, the pleasures of life and free love are extolled, and the birth of a child was considered to be the least desirable consequence.

It is a strange paradox that in the Graeco-Roman world of this same period something like a rediscovery of the child occurred. Although the Emperor Augustus did not allow the child of his granddaughter, Julia, to be reared, he is nevertheless described as a friend of children. Children were bought at slave markets to become the pets of adults to amuse them at their feasts. The child was rediscovered as a poetic figure. Also, painters and sculptors now became sensitive to the special physiology of children who were depicted as cupids or as playing with animals. Stories about children became the fashion in the parlours of the patrician families in Rome.

Towards the end of the 1st century A.D., Quintilian from Spain attempted to reform the savage school system in Rome. In his *Institutio Oratoria*, he outlined his educational ideals which were based on a firm belief in the child. Therefore, he demanded the highest qualities of a nurse and of teachers, and he severely condemned all the flogging which had become daily routine in Roman schools. The child's "studies must be made an amusement: he must be questioned and praised and taught to rejoice when he has done well; sometimes, too, when he refuses instruction, it should be given to some other to excite his envy; at times, also, he must be engaged in competition and should be allowed to believe himself successful more often than not, while he should be encouraged to do his best by such rewards as may appeal to his tender years" (*Institutio Oratoria* I, 1, 20).

But even more than through such educational ideals, children became centres of interest because they served as important religious mediums. They were considered to be chaste, to have no sexual complications and therefore to be innocent. True, children were also seen to share in the universality of human imperfection and guilt. But because they still lacked a sense of discernment, children were not held responsible for what they did. Moreover, due to their state of sexual innocence, they were thought to be especially beloved of the gods and could therefore act as intermediaries. Thus, a children's procession for special requests to the gods was considered to be particularly efficacious. Children acted as mediums in magic practices, too.

The religious significance of children led to stories about the divine child. Miracles were said to have been accomplished by men such as Alexander the Great or Emperor Augustus during their childhood. The child, Dionysus, and the naughty boy, Eros, became beloved themes of poets and artists. Above all, the hope for a better future crystallized itself in the hope of the coming of a divine child. Thus, the Roman poet, Virgil, dedicated in 40 B.C. his famous fourth eclogue to his protector, the Consul Pollio. There, he combined the ancient myth of the golden age with the birth of a divine-human boy:

> "Now is come the last age of the Song of Cumae; the great line of the centuries begins anew. Now the Virgin returns, the reign of Saturn returns; now a new generation descends from heaven on high. Only do thou, pure Lucina, smile on the birth of the child, under whom the iron brood shall first cease, and a golden race spring up throughout the world! Thine own Apollo now is king! And in thy consulship, Pollio, yea in thine, shall this glorious age begin, and the mighty months commence their march; under thy sway, any lingering traces of our guilt shall become void, and release the earth from its continual dread. He shall have the gift of divine life, shall see heroes mingled with gods, and shall himself be seen of them, and shall sway a world to which his father's virtues have brought peace. But for thee, child, shall the earth untilled pour forth, as her first pretty gifts,...." (*Eclogue* IV, 4-20).

The child among the Jews

According to the Old Testament, children are a precious gift from God. Far from being disposable as in the Graeco-Roman world, children in the Jewish world are received as a blessing. "Lo, sons are a heritage from the Lord, the fruit of the womb, a reward. Like arrows in the hand of a warrior are the sons of one's youth. Happy is the man who has his quiver full of them!" (Ps. 127 : 3-5).

Begetting and giving birth to children is an order of creation under God's special blessing (Gen. 1 : 28), and fertility forms an essential part of God's promise to Abraham and his people (Gen. 12 : 3). Thus, the exodus, the key event in Israel's history of salvation, begins with a miraculous fertility of Israelite women which defeats all of Pharaoh's drastic counter measures (Ex. 1-2). Mothers of many children are therefore called blessed (Gen. 24 : 60), while childlessness is considered a curse. The prayers of Hannah are telling examples of both the misery of barrenness and great thankfulness for the gift of a child (I Sam. 1). Special laws and customs safeguarded the continuation of the family. If a married man died without having a son, the husband's brother was bound to take the widow as his wife so that a son be born and his brother's name continued (Deut. 25 : 5-10). A barren woman could give one of her maids to her husband so that through her she may have children (Gen. 30 : 1-13). Conversely, contraception was considered to be infamous. (Gen. 38 : 8 ff.). The Roman historian, Tacitus, testifies that child exposure was unknown among Jews and that "they regard it as a crime to kill any late-born child" (*Histories* 5.5).

This great desire for the precious gift of children arose from the people of Israel's strong feeling of having been chosen and called by their God for a special task. As members of the people of the Covenant, Israelites felt bound to continue their presence on earth. A land had been promised and entrusted to them, and therefore it was necessary to safeguard future offspring so that this earth would be tilled. The God of Abraham, Isaac and Jacob had revealed to them his *Torah*, that is, his will and precepts. This made it imperative that there always be Israelites to worship this God and walk according to his *Torah* among the nations. It was primarily this need to continue the race which caused children to be considered such a precious gift.

Outside this context of the Covenant, the land and the *Torah*, the children as such had no special importance. Like the literature of other people, so also the Old Testament bears witness to paternal and maternal love (for example, Gen. 22 : 2; I Kings 3 : 26). Yet the Israelites did not idealize children, nor did they pay any special attention to the children's individuality. Infants, boys and girls, were part of the people. Already on the eighth day boys were circumcised to become a visible part of the Covenant (Gen. 17 : 12) and from early childhood onwards children participated in family worship and the great celebrations of the Covenant. In the period before the Babylonian exiles, there were no schools nor any religious education specially programmed and adapted for children. They had to learn by living, praying and working with their parents.

Nothing is said in the Old Testament about the innocence of children. Once, "the child quieted at its mother's breast" is used as a parable for peace (Ps. 131 : 2). Even babes and infants can praise God (Ps. 8 : 2), and exceptionally a boy like Samuel received the gift of prophecy (I Sam. 3 : 1-9). As elsewhere in the ancient world, the expected Saviour is sometimes visualized as a child (Isa. 7 : 14 ff; 9 : 5 ff.). Yet, according to Jewish belief, the children need atonement no less than their parents, "for the imagination of man's heart is evil from his youth" (Gen. 8 : 21), and an Israelite could pray: "Behold, I was brought forth in iniquity, and in sin did my mother conceive me" (Ps. 51 : 5). If anything, children symbolize lack of understanding. Woe to the city which is ruled by a mere boy (Isa. 3 : 4; Eccl. 10 : 16). God's judgment falls on adults and children alike. "Their infants will be dashed in pieces before their eyes; their houses will be plundered and their wives ravished" (Isa. 13 : 16). The prophet Elijah, obviously lacking any sense of humour, showed no mercy to the naughty boys who made fun of his baldness: "He cursed them in the name of the Lord. And two she-bears came out of the woods and tore forty-two of the boys" (II Kings 2 : 24).

The one commandment which ruled the whole life of children and young people was: "Honour your father and your mother"; "Cursed be he who dishonours his father or his mother" (Ex. 20 : 12; Deut. 27 : 16). As gifts from God, children were only entrusted to their parents. The first-born in particular belonged to God, had especially to be presented to him, and be redeemed by a sacrifice. Yet, though only trustees, the parents represented God himself, and their authority came immediately after God's. According to the *Talmud*, the rabbis later taught: "Three combine (in the making of) men: God and father and mother. If men honour their father and mother, God says, 'I reckon it to them as if I dwelt among them, and as if they honoured me' " (*Kiddushin* 30b). According to the deuteronomic legislation, the punishment for a rebellious son was no less than lapidation (Deut. 21 : 18-21).

No wonder that, in the Old Testament, the technical term for education is *jasar*, which originally meant "to flog", "to chastise", "to discipline". This disciplining and instruction is a favoured theme of the wisdom literature in the Old Testament, and intertestamental times: "Folly is bound up in the heart of a child, but the rod of discipline drives it far from him." "He who spares the rod hates his son, but he who loves him is diligent to discipline him" (Prov. 22 : 15; 13 : 24). The aim of this harsh instruction is the "fear of God" (Prov. 1 : 7). This expression could perhaps be better translated with "the awe before God", for it means the confident and obedient submission under the will of God as manifested in the *Torah*.

The Jewish rabbis, in the time of Jesus and the centuries there-after, continued to emphasize this all important relationship between the children and the *Torah*. The schools were totally devoted to the reading, memorizing and understanding of the one and only text book — the Hebrew Bible. In this connection, no attributes high enough could be found for children: Rabbi Hamnuna (4th century A.D.) said: "Jerusalem was destroyed only because the children did not attend school, and loitered in the streets" (*Sabbath* 119b). It was preoccupation with the *Torah*, and not any innate qualities of children, which justified such a high appreciation of their role. Taken by themselves, the children had, also among the rabbis, no higher status than that described in the Old Testament. Obedience to parents and teachers was equally strongly emphasized, and when necessary the rod was used for disciplining them.

Some rabbis held that a child aged less than a year old was not yet responsible, and for some others this applied to children of up to nine years of age. To a certain degree, these children were therefore considered to be sinless. It could even be stated that "God said: 'As the sacrifices are pure, so are children pure'" (*Pesikta Kahana* 60b/61a). Yet other rabbis, however, debated the question of whether children did not already sin in the womb. Also, the question of whether or not children of the ungodly in the land of Israel would partake of the coming resurrection was much debated. On the whole, children outside the school were considered insignificant. In enumerations, they appear together with women. Matthew was certainly not the only Jew who did not count them at all when he reported about the miraculous feeding of the five thousand: "those who ate were about five thousand men, besides women and children" (Matt. 14 : 21). For a scholar to play with children and spend time with them outside his teaching period was regarded as a waste of time. This, anyhow, was the opinion of rabbi Dosa ben Harkinas (ca. 90 A.D.) which is reported in the *Mishna:* "Morning sleep and mid-day wine and children's talk and sitting in the meeting-houses of the ignorant people put a man out of the world" (*Aboth* 3, 11).

Lest someone should mistakenly think that the rabbis had no sense of humour and that the poor Jewish children were never allowed to play, it is good to add the following story. It shows that rabbis were human enough to act from time to time against their own convictions: "There was once a man who made a will saying that his son should inherit nothing of his till he became a fool. Rabbi Jose ben

Judah and rabbi Judah the Prince went to rabbi Joshua ben Karha to ask about this matter. They saw him outside his house, and noticed that he was crawling on his hands and feet with a reed in his mouth, and following his son. When they saw him, they hid themselves, and then they went to him, and asked him about the will. He laughed and said, 'The matter about which you ask has happened to me'. Hence you see that when a man loves to have children, he acts like a fool' " (*Midrash* Ps. 92, 14. 206b, § 13. The rabbis mentioned lived in the 2nd century A.D.).

An Aramaic paraphrase of Exodus 15 : 2 shows that even rabbis could learn from children. The *Targum* comments on the fact that infants often move the fingers of their little hands while drinking at their mother's breast. This gesture is interpreted as sign language addressed to their earthly fathers: "From the breast of (their) mothers, sucklings made signs with their fingers to their fathers and said to them: 'He is our Father who gave us honey to suck out of the rock, and gave us oil from the flinty rock' " (*Targum Yerushalmi* to Exodus 15 : 2).

Jesus and the children

Seen against this background of Graeco-Roman and Jewish attitudes to children, what was Jesus' attitude? He was a Jew, and obviously what the Old Testament and the Jewish intertestamental writings reveal about children was much more important for him than what Greek and Roman educators and philosophers thought about the matter.

It is true that, in Jesus' time, the Graeco-Roman and the Jewish world very much interpenetrated and influenced one another. However, Jesus was not like his contemporary, Philon, the Jewish philosopher in Alexandria, who attempted to build a bridge between these two worlds. Nor can He be understood simply as part of the Jewish-rabbinic world. In his acts and words, something deeply Jewish and, at the same time, radically new appeared. This manifested itself also in the actions and sayings of Jesus when He received children into his company. As will be shown in the following chapters, Jesus' attitude to children was so new and astonishing that his disciples could not grasp it. One even wonders whether the Christian Church since then has fully understood these amazing actions and sayings which will now be explored.

At the very outset of this search for understanding, it is important to recall the parable of the children's game. This parable and its application show that Jesus did not idealize children. In that particular case, He saw in their game which went wrong an exemplary instance of how "this generation" fails to discern what really matters.

Thus, Jesus had a fully realistic view of children. Yet, in his originality, He always confronted such human views of people and events with the realism of God's Kingdom. This led not only to new teaching, but to Christians confessing that in the person of Jesus — in his teaching, life, death and resurrection — God's Kingdom was actually anticipated. Within this anticipated reality of the Kingdom, children appear in a totally new light.

2 · Let the Children Come to Me

The Story Behind Mark 10 : 13-16

When Jesus entered Jerusalem, riding on a young donkey, people of that city asked: "Who is this?" They got a quick answer from the crowds who had just shouted their hosannah: "This is the prophet, Jesus from Nazareth of Galilee!" (Matt. 21 : 10 ff.).

The touch of a prophet

In the eyes of the Jews in Palestine, Jesus was in the first instance a rabbi. Like other teachers, He gathered disciples and explained the Scriptures, teaching what was God's will for everyday life. Yet this rabbi did not teach like the others. Moreover, He healed and performed miracles. Gradually, therefore, the crowds began to see him as a prophet, though He never called himself this.

What exactly people meant when they called Jesus a prophet cannot be ascertained. There were prophets among the Pharisees and Essenes at that time. Through the power of the Spirit, they had extraordinary insights. They could interpret dreams, penetrate men's hidden thoughts and announce the meaning of future events. The Samaritan woman had obviously seen Jesus as such a prophet. (John 4 : 19; cf. Luke 7 : 39 and Mark 6 : 15; 8 : 28). Yet people must sometimes have wondered whether Jesus was not more than that. Should He not rather be compared with "one of the old prophets" of Old Testament times (Luke 9 : 8; cf. Luke 9 : 19; Matt. 16 : 14)? He taught as one who had authority, rather like the great prophets who announced: "Thus says the Lord". Moreover, his mighty acts must have led at least some among the crowds to ask whether He was not *the* prophet. Would not Elijah be sent back to earth during the last days, in order "to turn the hearts of fathers to their children and the hearts of children to their fathers", as Malachi had announced (Mal. 4 : 5 ff.)? Had not Moses himself made this great promise: "The

Lord your God will raise up for you a prophet like me from among you" (Deut. 18 : 15-20)? Some people actually said that Jesus was Elijah (Mark 6 : 15; 8 : 28), and after the miraculous feeding of the multitude, people responded to this sign with the acknowledgment: "This is indeed the prophet who is to come into the world!" (John 6 : 14; cf. Luke 7 : 16).

Whatever meaning was given to the term "prophet", the crowd met in Jesus an extraordinary rabbi, a divine man. No wonder, therefore, that children were brought to him so that He might touch them.

There was a custom of children asking for the blessing of famous rabbis, just as sons and daughters went to their father to be blessed. In *Soferim*, one of the late minor tracts which are included in some editions of the *Talmud*, the following information is given: "It was a beautiful custom in Jerusalem to make the little children, boys and girls, fast on the fast-day (that is, on the Day of Atonement), those who were a year old until daybreak, the twelve-year-olds till evening, and then carry or lead them to the elders (the scribes) for them to bless them, strengthen (that is, exhort) and pray for them, that they might one day attain to knowledge of the *Torah* and to good works" (*Soferim* 18.5). As with most rabbinic writings, one can no more ascertain how far back the oral tradition concerning this information reaches. It is quite possible that, in Jesus' day, this custom already existed and that it was followed not only in Jerusalem, but also in the cities and villages of Galilee. One could imagine, therefore, that the scene described in Mark 10 : 13 ff. happened on the evening of a Day of Atonement, although this is far from certain. If so, it is most revealing to compare what Jesus did and said on that occasion with what is reported about blessing by the elders.

The children were not only brought to be blessed. According to Mark's and Luke's account, they were brought "that He may touch them". This request probably meant more than the customary blessing. In the four gospels, almost all of the more than 30 occurrences of the verb "to touch" are found in stories where Jesus heals lepers, the blind or the sick. The healing touch of this prophet from Nazareth must have become proverbial. Even healthy people expected a special benediction from Jesus' touch, and therefore children were brought to him. Yet the disciples would not let it happen, which provoked Jesus' indignation (cf. Worksheet II in Appendix D).

This is the only place in the whole New Testament where it is written that Jesus was indignant. Jesus could be deeply moved (Mark 1 : 41), He sometimes would sternly rebuke someone (Mark 1 : 43) or even be full of anger (Mark 3 : 5). But here, He is indignant, and in his indignation Jesus addresses himself to quite another group than his disciples had expected.

The evangelists do not tell who brought the children. Christian artists usually depict mothers carrying babies in their arms (Luke in fact writes about *brephē*, the Greek term for babies) together with elder children led by their mother's hand. However, none of the three parallel accounts of the evanglists mentions any women, and the presence of women in the gospels is usually specially emphasized. The children came probably with their fathers or more likely with their elder brothers and sisters. These were rebuked by the disciples.

Again, the evangelists do no not specify why the disciples felt it necessary to hinder the children from coming. Were these children ritually unclean? Did the disciples, as typical Jews of their time, consider children too insignificant to take up the time and attention of their master? Was their intention to resist an almost magic belief in the power of the prophet's touch? We do not know. We can be certain, however, that the disciples were astonished about their master's reaction. Instead of being indignant with those who brought the children Jesus became indignant with his well-meaning disciples!

Earlier Peter had been put straight in a similarly harsh manner. When Jesus had announced his coming suffering and death, Peter rebuked his master, presumably advising him not to go the way of the cross. Yet this rebuke was immediately returned: Jesus "rebuked Peter, and said, 'Get behind me, Satan! For you are not on the side of God, but of men' " (Mark 8 : 33). This was followed up with an important teaching about discipleship. Just as during that crucial conversation near Caesarea Philippi the disciples were not "on God's side" and had therefore to be taught the true way of discipleship, so it happened now when they hindered the children from coming to him. The whole sequence of events recalls yet another incident where, again, the disciples did not perceive what really mattered and had to be taught through a meaningful gesture and word: In the house of Simon the leper at Bethany a woman came with an alabaster jar of very costly ointment. She broke that jar in order to anoint Jesus. In this case, some of the bystanders, presumably the disciples, became indignant and they reproached the woman (Mark 14 : 3-5). Yet, just as during the incident with the children, Jesus intervened with literally the same command: "Let be!" (in Greek *aphete*), "Let her alone; why do you trouble her?... She has anointed my body beforehand for burying. And truly, I say to you, wherever the Gospel is preached in the whole world, what she has done will be told in memory of her" (Mark 14 : 6-9). Indeed, it is in such extraordinary actions and sayings in the midst of everyday scenes of life with seemingly unimportant people like women and children that the very core of the Gospel is revealed.

A prophetic word and act

It is difficult to know exactly what Jesus said when children were brought to him. Mark, Matthew and Luke almost totally agree with regard to the first saying which fits in very well with what had been told so far: "Let the children come to me, do not hinder them; for to such belongs the Kingdom of God" (Mark 10 : 14). Matthew then immediately concludes the passage by briefly referring to Jesus' gesture of the laying on of hands. Mark and Luke add another saying of Jesus which interrupts the main line of thought. The passage speaks about Jesus' attitude to children and their relationship to God's Kingdom. The saying of Mark 10 : 15, however, refers figuratively to the children as an example in discipleship. Moreover, Matthew has used another version of presumably the same saying in the context of a different passage where Jesus does in fact present a child as an example of discipleship (Matt. 18 : 3). A similar saying of Jesus is reported by John in yet another context (John 3 : 3, 5). Jesus may, of course, have taught his disciples on different occasions that in order to enter the Kingdom one must receive it like a child. However, He was too good a teacher to make two different points on one and the same occasion. If one attempts to replace the story behind Mark 10 : 13-16 in its original setting, it is advisable to leave out the second saying of Jesus (Mark 10 : 15), which was probably inserted later from another context.

With regard to Jesus' actions, we can be almost certain that Mark reports what actually happened. Not all interpreters would agree with this statement. Some believe that the earliest Church originally knew only a saying of Jesus concerning the children (Mark 10 : 14b, possibly a further development of the saying in Mark 9 : 37). According to them, it was the Church which, during the period of oral transmission, created for this saying the context of the scene in which the disciples rebuke those who want to bring children to Jesus (Mark

10 : 13-14a). That incident should not, then, be understood as something which actually happened, but rather as an ideal scene, a biographical note to introduce the saying of Jesus. The same interpreters also believe that Mark later added the end of the story (Mark 10 : 16).

Contrary to the above understanding of how the story grew, it seems much more likely that the scene, the first saying of Jesus and his actions belonged together from the beginning. Jesus lived and taught in an oral culture, where actions and sayings went together. It was in this way that the Old Testament prophets announced God's will. Similarly, during his last supper, Jesus taught the disciples with both actions and words (John 13 : 1-20; Mark 14 : 22-25). He did so earlier, too, when children were brought to him. In all these cases, the deeds are more than mere illustrations of the sayings, and the words much more than explanations of the deeds. In different, yet complementary ways, the two together communicate the message.

Those who brought the children wanted Jesus to touch them. He did so, although the ominous verb "to touch" is not used again at the end of the story. In fact, the way in which Jesus spoke to the children and sought physical contact with them, far surpassed what was expected, and must therefore have astonished both the disciples and those who had brought the children.

Having set his disciples straight, Jesus made a surprising announcement. In the original setting, He probably did not say: "To people who are like such children belongs the Kingdom of God". In this case, the children would serve as a metaphor. Jesus did sometimes use such figurative language with regard to children, as will be shown in chapter three. Moreover, from the time of Mark onwards, the evangelists have indeed understood Jesus' sayings in this metaphorical way. However, in the original setting, Jesus referred to the actual children which were brought to him. The original Aramaic must therefore have said: "To these and other such children belongs the Kingdom of God."

Some interpreters have wondered whether Jesus wanted to say thereby that these children would witness the establishment of God's Kingdom. Would these boys and girls under 13 be the generation of the last times, those "who will not taste death before they see that the Kingdom of God has come with power" (Mark 9 : 1)? Nothing in the text itself suggests such a reference to future events. On the contrary, the saying and the actions which followed immediately afterwards confirm that Jesus spoke about a present reality. On the evening of the Day of Atonement, a rabbi might have blessed the children and exhorted them to go to school and learn diligently, so that some time in the future they might know the *Torah* and be enabled to do good works. Jesus also blessed the children. He gave a sermon as well, although that was not addressed to the children, but to the adults. At that very moment, the children received the greatest gift possible, the Kingdom of God, which is both a present and a future reality.

Jesus immediately symbolized this gift by taking the children in his arms. The Greek term used for this occurs only twice in the New Testament, and both times with regard to children (Mark 10 : 16 and Mark 9 : 36). It recalls the scene in which Simeon took up the child, Jesus, in his arms (Luke 2 : 28) and when, in the parable of the two sons, the father embraced and kissed the prodigal son who had returned home. In the story about the children, this gesture of tenderness and protection becomes the counterpart to the indignation of Jesus. There is more than a magic touch here. The symbolic action is deeply significant. According to a rabbinic treatise, the resurrection of the people of Israel will happen when "God embraces them, presses them to his heart and kisses them, thus bringing them into the life of the world to come" (*Seder Elijahu Rabba* 17). Something like that has happened to the children. They who received the Kingdom were embraced by the messianic king.

How did the children merit such a reception? Absolutely no condition is made. The children have not yet reached even "the age of the Law", and they therefore have no merit. Nothing is said about their innocence, their childlike confidence or any other such qualities. If anything is suggested at all in the text, it is the children's helplessness and weakness, for they must be brought to Jesus. But the main point of Jesus' prophetic words and action does not lie here. What He intended to teach was not something about the nature of children. Rather, He wanted to reveal the nature of God. God's will is to present the children with his Kingdom, and against all human calculation this is done in a totally gratuitous way. Thus, children are counted among the poor in spirit who have been called blessed because "theirs is the Kingdom of Heaven" (Matt. 5 : 3). It has pleased God to do so, without any reasons being given. His love for children is as "unreasonable" as the generosity of the steward in the parable of the labourers in the vineyard (Matt. 20 : 1-20).

This gratuitous love of God, assured to the children in Jesus' prophetic words and action, turns upside down both Greek and

Jewish classifications. Children receive a place of preeminence, if human realities are considered from the point of view of God's Kingdom.

A baptismal text?

Stories have their own life. It is not possible to fix them once and for all in just one particular milieu. So far, we have examined how the story behind Mark 10 : 13-16 is rooted in the historical setting of Jesus' life and teaching. In that original setting, the events reported as well as Jesus' saying and gestures have nothing to do with baptism.

The fact remains, however, that from the Middle Ages onwards this story became part of many baptismal liturgies. Since the confrontation with Anabaptists at the time of the Reformation — and only since then — has the story of Jesus' reception of the children also played an important role in the debate about children's baptism. The later influences of Mark 10 : 13-16 fall outside the scope of this study. It is possible, however, that this passage had a prehistory related to baptism. It has been suggested that the story of Jesus and the children was taken into the oral tradition and was preserved as such because it confirmed the early Church in its practice of children's baptism. This hypothesis can neither be proved nor disproved in a clear-cut way. None of the New Testament texts on baptism explicitly refers to children, and conversely none of the New Testament texts on children refers explicitly to baptism.

There are words and deeds in Mark 10 : 13-16 which make association of this story with baptism possible. The converted Ethiopian eunuch asked the evangelist Philip: "What is to prevent my being baptized?" (Acts 8 : 36). The Greek verb *kōlyein* ("to prevent", "to hinder") used both in this text and in Jesus' reprimand to his disciples in Mark 10 : 14a appears elsewhere in connection with baptism (Acts 10 : 47; 11 : 17; *dia-kōlyein* in Matt. 3 : 14). It is possible that this was a technical term in early Christian baptismal formulas. As in the Jewish baptism of proselytes, so also in the early Christian baptism candidates were tested beforehand in order to ascertain whether anything prevented them from being accepted into the community of the faithful. In this connection, Jesus' saying in Mark 10 : 14 could well be used as an argument for the baptism of children. Also Jesus' action of laying on of hands (Mark 10 : 16) would then have been interpreted as a reference to the baptismal rite. Moreover, the second saying of Jesus (Mark 10 : 15) was probably related early on to the rebirth of water and the Spirit in baptism, as its parallel in John 3 : 5 suggests.

The above arguments point indeed to the possibility that, during the period of oral tradition, the story behind Mark 10 : 13-16 was associated with the practice of children's baptism. Yet there are equally valid counter-arguments. In the New Testament, the verb *kōlyein* is more frequently used in passages which do not speak about baptism at all (for example, Mark 9 : 39). Its presumed technical significance in relation to baptism therefore remains doubtful. It is also not certain whether the above-mentioned second saying of Jesus (Mark 10 : 15) became part of the story during the period of oral tradition. Moreover, in John 3 : 3 and 5, the allusion to baptism relates to being given rebirth from above. This condition for entering the Kingdom is different from that in Mark 10 : 15. The Johannine version of Jesus' saying cannot, therefore, be directly used to relate the story behind Mark 10 : 13-16 to children's baptism. The strongest counter–argument is the fact that, when Mark finally wrote down the story and inserted it in his gospel, he made no reference to baptism. As will be shown in the next chapter, for Mark, Matthew and Luke the point of the story lay elsewhere.

In view of these arguments and counter-arguments, it can no longer be ascertained whether or not the early Church did, in fact, relate this story to children's baptism. If it did, it must have faced the same dilemma as the Church has done ever since. The story has been used to impress on parents that they *must* bring their children to be baptized. Baptism is then seen as an absolute prerequisite for receiving salvation and for participating in God's Kingdom. In this way, the story receives a legalistic overtone which contradicts its original meaning. As was pointed out earlier, Jesus' prophetic words and deeds radically reject such legalistic reckonings along with prerequisites and merits. Whatever the motives of those who brought the children, whatever may be the condition of the children — we might perhaps add: whether they are baptized or not — "to such belongs the Kingdom of God". Precisely this free gift of God's love can also be expressed through children's baptism. Wherever the baptism of children is taught and practised as such, not as "cheap grace" but as a procla- mation of God's costly grace, there the story of Jesus' reception of the children is understood in its original meaning.

3 · Unless You Become Like a Child

Mark 10:15; Luke 18:17; Matt. 18:3

As Jesus walked through the countryside and cities of Galilee, He saw many sights. Here, He saw a man sowing good seed. There, He observed preparations for a marriage feast. Further on, a woman was mixing yeast with flour. At another place, He heard the angry voice of a labourer shouting to another: "Pay back what you owe me!" Many such everyday activities and events became Jesus' parables of the Kingdom. "The Kingdom of God is like...".

The language of metaphors

Parables were not an invention of Jesus. In his time, they had become a means of instruction among the rabbis. In rabbinic discussions, parables usually served as illustrative stories in teaching or as a means of making a point in a debate to impress it firmly on the mind of the opponent. Both the Old and the New Testament contain examples of this kind of pedagogical and polemic use of parables. Thus, the short parable of the children playing in the market place which we studied earlier is a good example of the polemic use of parables.

In Jesus' parables of the Kingdom, however, there is a special new quality. They can best be characterized as extended metaphors. A metaphor is more than a simple comparison. In the latter, something less known is illustrated and clarified by something better known. Thus, in the earlier mentioned parable of the children in the market place, the behaviour of "this generation" is compared with the behaviour of children who do not know the game or even spoil the game. The parable there just helps to clarify and illustrate what people do in the decisive hour when John the Baptist and Jesus come. The metaphor also makes a comparison, but this is done not by way of illustration, but by way of evocation. A metaphor shocks the imagination of the hearer or reader, because two not entirely comparable elements are juxtaposed. Thus, a new vision of reality is opened up by making ordinary things and events in nature and everyday life reflect the ultimate reality of God's Kingdom.

Metaphors and their extended forms — the parables of the Kingdom — contain their message in themselves. Usually, something odd appears in the story, which strangely breaks through the normal pattern. This strangeness may be a sudden change of roles, an astonishing turn of events or unexpected results. Such parables cannot be explained with sentences like: "The whole point of the story is. . ." The evocative nature of these parables leaves them open-ended. It defies any attempt to state once and for all the intended meaning. Instead of transmitting such a definite teaching about the Kingdom of God, the parables of the Kingdom draw listeners and readers into a learning process. The audience is invited to participate, to become part of the metaphor of the parable story.

Without understanding this language of metaphors, one cannot perceive the meaning of Jesus' saying about a child in Mark 10 : 15 and its parallels. For here — contrary to verses 14 and 16 in Mark 10 — the "child" has become a metaphor.

Receiving and entering the Kingdom

Jesus' words in Mark 10 : 15 and Luke 18 : 17 must originally have been an independent saying of the Lord. The saying in Matthew 18 : 3 and perhaps also that in John 3 : 3, 5 probably come out of the same tradition. The original occasion on which Jesus pronounced this saying and its original wording can no longer be determined. There are many instances of such unattached sayings of Jesus. In the oral tradition, they "floated" for a certain time before becoming attached to a given historic context or being integrated into an appropriate story. This happened also with Jesus' saying about receiving and entering the Kingdom (cf. Worksheet III in Appendix D). Mark and Luke transmit this saying in exactly identical wording as part of the story of Jesus who lets the children come to him. Matthew transmits another wording and places the saying into the context of the scene where the disciples ask who is the greatest in the Kingdom and where Jesus puts a child in the midst of them. John reports a similar saying of Jesus in yet another version as part of the conversation between Jesus and Nicodemus.

A late development of perhaps the same saying of Jesus appears in a fifth gospel, namely, the apocryphal gospel of Thomas. It was written in the 2nd century A.D. and was found in Egypt some decades ago. This gospel contains 114 "secret words which the living Jesus spoke", as its introduction claims. All these sayings remain unattached one to another. Generally, they are simply introduced with the expression "Jesus said" and only very seldom are they set into the context of a scene in Jesus' life. They have many parallels to sayings of Jesus in the canonical gospels. The 22nd word reads as follows:

> "Jesus saw some infants at the breast. He said to his disciples: 'These little ones at the breast are like those who enter into the Kingdom.' They said to him: 'If we then be children, shall we enter the Kingdom?' Jesus said to them: 'When you make two one, and when you make the inside as the outside, and the outside as the inside, and the upper side as the lower; and when you make the male and the female into a single one, that the male be not male and the female female; when you make eyes in the place of an eye, and a hand in the place of a hand, and a foot in place of a foot, an image in place of an image, then you shall enter (the Kingdom)' ".

This saying makes the same point as that in Mark 10 : 15 and its parallels: the child is used as a metaphor, and the disciples are taught that they can enter the Kingdom only if they become like a child. What it means to be a child is spelled out here in a rather obscure way, which shows influences from the hellenistic concept that children are not conscious of their sexuality and are therefore sexually innocent. This is confirmed by another of the secret words in the gospel of Thomas: "His disciples said: 'On what day wilt thou be revealed to us, and on what day shall we see thee?' Jesus said: 'When you unclothe yourselves and are not ashamed, and take your garments and lay them beneath your feet like little children'..." (*Logion* 37). Such sayings show above all the great distance between the Jesus of the gospel of Thomas and the Jesus as we come to know him in the canonical gospels. It is to the latter's saying that we now return.

"Truly, I say unto you". This solemn beginning emphasizes the character of trustworthy revelation. The prophets used to preface their utterances with the words: "Thus says the Lord". In this instance, Jesus assumes God's authority. He is more than a prophet; He guarantees with his own person and ministry the truth of the announcement like He does in other sayings about the Kingdom (cf. for example, Mark 9 : 41; 10 : 29; 13 : 30; 14 : 25).

"Whoever does not receive the Kingdom of God like a child..." In the gospels, the verb "to receive" is used almost exclusively for receiving somebody, for the act of hospitality: children (Mark 9: 27), the disciples (Mark 6 : 11) or Jesus himself (Mark 9 : 37) are received. In Acts and the New Testament letters, the verb is sometimes used in the same way (for example, Gal. 4 : 14), but more often it refers to receiving "the Word of God" (Acts 8 : 14; 11 : 1; I Thess. 1 : 6, and others), the "gospel" (II Cor. 11 : 4), the "grace of God" (II Cor. 6: 1) or similar gifts from God. Only in this saying is the Kingdom the object received. Some scholars are therefore of the opinion that this expression betrays the language of the Church rather than that of Jesus. Consequently, Mark's and Luke's versions are considered to be secondary. Matthew's version is held to be closer to the original saying.

Whether this is so or not, the meaning of the expression about "receiving the Kingdom" must still be explained. Should one paraphrase: "whoever does not receive the message of the Kingdom..." or "whoever does not receive me..."? Both paraphrases say too little. Jesus does not speak here only about the message of the coming Kingdom or specifically about himself. The Kingdom itself is seen here as a present reality which can be given or taken away (cf. Matt. 16 : 19; 21 : 43; Luke 12 : 32), which can be received or lost.

While the expression "to receive the Kingdom of God" is unique in New Testament literature, it may well have been current in Jesus' time and environment. This can be inferred from such later rabbinical sayings as the following. Rabbi Judah said in the name of Rab (Rab Abba Areka lived from 160 to 247 A.D.): "He who has to say the *Shema* while he is out walking must stand still, and receive the Kingdom of heaven. And what is the Kingdom of Heaven? The Lord our God, the Lord is One" (*Deuteronomy Rabbah* 2.31). To receive the Kingdom is here equated with the recital of the first part of the *Shema*. This is the basic Jewish prayer and watchword (a combination of Deut. 6 : 4-9 with Deut. 11 : 13-21 and later also Num. 15 : 37-47). It implies total submission under God's kingship. This *Shema* has to be prayed twice a day by every believing Jew, and the Jerusalem *Talmud* prescribes: "How is a wayfarer to pray? He must not take the Kingdom of Heaven upon himself while he is walking, but he must pause, direct his heart to God with awe and fear, trembling and quaking, at the proclamation of the divine unity, as he utters the *Shema*, every single word with heartfelt sincerity, and then he should recite the doxology. But when he begins the following paragraph,

he may, if he so desires, resume his journey and pray as he walks..."
(*Tanhuma, Lekleka* § 1, f, 24a; date uncertain, 2nd or 3rd century
A.D.).

Thus, a child could receive the Kingdom only if it obediently
learned to pray the *Shema*. In fact, as soon as a boy could speak,
"his father teaches him the *Shema*, *Torah* and the sacred tongue;
otherwise, it were better he had not come into the world" (*Tosefta
Hagigah* 1, 2). Could it be that, with the saying about the child and
the Kingdom, Jesus has challenged the then perhaps already current
rabbinical concept of how the Kingdom of Heaven is to be received?
If so, He has set the metaphor of the child in the place of the liturgical
practice of reciting the *Shema*.

Before examining the second part of the sentence, it is important
to listen also to Matthew's version which may, in fact, be nearer to
Jesus' original saying than Mark's and Luke's version. After the
introductory formula, Jesus said, according to Matthew: "unless you
turn and become like children..." Is this a call to conversion? Many
Bible translators and exegetes have understood the meaning of the
verb "turn" in this way. The Greek word used, *strephein*, has indeed
the same root as the current New Testament verb for the act of conversion, *epistrephein*. Yet, in the twenty-one occurrences of the verb
strephein in the New Testament, it almost always means to physically
turn around towards somebody (for example, Matt. 5 : 39; 7 : 6;
9 : 22). Except in one Old Testament quotation cited in John 12 : 40,
the verb never designates religious conversion. Moreover the saying
is addressed to the disciples who have already become believers. Jesus
does not speak about how one can enter into the community of
believers, but about what is expected of members of this community
in order that they may reach the goal of their vocation. For the same
reason, it is also problematic to use John's version of the saying ("unless
one is born anew/from above..." John 3 : 3) to explain Matthew's
version. Neither a rebirth and a return to one's original state of childhood is asked for, nor a religious conversion. Rather, Jesus calls a
halt to the disciples who had spent much time on the question of who
is the greatest in the Kingdom of Heaven. They must learn to think
differently about their relationship to the Kingdom. They must turn
around and no longer look out for the greatest, but see the little ones;
in Matthew's context: the child which Jesus had put into their midst.

"... shall not enter the Kingdom of Heaven". In Jesus' teaching,
this expression always relates to the last judgment, and it is connected

with stern exhortations and a call to a new way of life in the here and now: "Unless your righteousness exceeds that of the Scribes and Pharisees, you will never enter the Kingdom of Heaven" (Matt. 5 : 20; cf. Matt. 7 : 21). "If your eye causes you to sin, pluck it out; it is better for you to enter the Kingdom of God with one eye than with two eyes to be thrown into hell" (Mark 9 : 47). After the conversation with the rich young man, where it becomes clear how hard it is to enter the Kingdom, the disciples lose heart and ask: "Then who can be saved?" And Jesus answers: "With men it is impossible, but not with God; for all things are possible with God" (Mark 10 : 23-27). It is this impossible thing which becomes possible for those who receive the Kingdom like a child, or who turn and become like a child.

The metaphor of the child

What does "like a child" mean in this context? This is a question with which interpreters have struggled throughout the centuries. If the term "child" is used here as a metaphor, we may not expect a definitive answer. Metaphors, after all, do not define meaning, but evoke it. They do not communicate a truth but issue an invitation to join a search for truth. It is, therefore, legitimate to suggest a rich variety of meanings, though — after testing — not all these meanings can be maintained.

The expression "like a child" can be understood as an accusative case. The saying must, then, be translated: "Whoever does not receive the Kingdom of God as one receives a child..." From a purely linguistic point of view, this interpretation is possible. As elsewhere in the gospels, the verb "to receive" would then be used for welcoming a person. Jesus would, in this case, state here for the Kingdom almost the same thing as he stated in Mark 9 : 37 for the reception of himself through the intermediary of a child. There are several considerations in favour of this interpretation. Understood in this way, verse 15 would no longer be an erratic block in the context of Mark 10 : 13-16. On the contrary, if the child can serve as a metaphor for God's Kingdom, it becomes all the more understandable why Jesus was indignant with his disciples and why He received the children so cordially and declared that "to such belongs the Kingdom". One can also cite a beautiful rabbinical passage in support of this interpretation, because there the *Shechinah* (the glorious manifestation of the presence of God) is linked with the presence of children. Rabbi Judah (middle of 2nd century A.D.) said: "See how beloved the little children are before

God. When the Sanhedrin went into captivity, the *Shechinah* went not with them; the watchers of the priests went into captivity; the *Shechinah* went not with them. But when the little children went into captivity, the *Shechinah* went with them. For it says in Lamentations 1 : 5: 'Her children are gone into captivity', and immediately after (1 : 6), 'From Zion her splendour is departed' " (*Lamentation Rabbah* 1,33). Despite such arguments for the acceptance of the above interpretation, the counter-arguments are more weighty. Nowhere else in the New Testament does a child serve as a metaphor for the Kingdom. The wording of this saying in both Matthew's and John's gospels excludes the above understanding. Moreover, if one studies the passages in Mark 10 : 13-16 and Luke 18 : 15-17 within their respective contexts, it becomes clear that these two evangelists, too, did not see the child as a metaphor of the Kingdom.

"Like a child" functions rather like a noun in the nominative case, and Jesus' saying must be translated: "Whoever does not receive the Kingdom of God like a child receives the Kingdom..." But then, what meanings are evoked by this metaphor? Especially Matthew's rendering ("unless you turn and become like children") leads to the question as to what the special qualities of being like a child might be. If one surveys the answers given by interpreters and preachers throughout the centuries, one is faced with an embarrassingly rich choice of qualities and conditions behind which the real child tends to disappear. Church Fathers have often idealized the child morally. They wrote, for instance, about the exemplary simplicity, humility and innocence of children. Other interpreters have since suggested that especially small children do not yet know evil, that they are full of trust, joy and obedience, that they do not yet calculate, but are open to all possibilities of life. More recently, much emphasis has been laid on the vulnerability of children, the fact that they are small and totally dependent on the care of adults and that they have no merits or demerits. Most of these interpretations emphasize the *being* of the child, as if Jesus had said: "Unless you receive the Kingdom of God like a child *is*..."

At least in Mark's and Luke's rendering of the saying, the metaphor does not evoke what a child *is*, but the way in which a child *receives* the Kingdom. If the saying is understood in this way — and this obviously corresponds best to Mark's and Luke's actual text — again several meanings are opened up. The accent can now be laid on the child as a metaphor of "objective humility". Children are not necessarily more humble than adults but being dependent, they look for help from adults as a matter of course. Thus, they are, in the first place, those who receive. As such, they become a metaphor of confident faith. To receive God's Kingdom like a child means to beg and claim this Kingdom like a child claims food and love. It means to receive with empty hands.

The accent can also be laid on the way in which God gives the Kingdom. He gives gratuitously, not to those who merit receiving it either because they have faithfully prayed the *Shema* or because they have achieved a high degree of spiritual maturity. The metaphor then shows — as the apostle Paul would say — that the Kingdom is given by grace alone, and that it can only be received through faith. This saying of Jesus acts as a counterbalance to his stern words, quoted earlier, about entering the Kingdom. These could be understood in the way in which the *Mishna* tract on the *Shema* explains:

> Rabbi Joshua ben Karha (ca. 150 A.D.) said: "Why does the section 'Hear, O Israel' precede 'And it shall come to pass if ye shall hearken?'. — So that a man may first take upon him the yoke of the Kingdom of Heaven and afterward take upon him the yoke of the commandments" (*Berakoth* 2, 2).

To enter the Kingdom is, then, seen first of all as a heavy yoke, a life-long struggle to achieve an even better righteousness than that of the Scribes and Pharisees. Yet such total obedience is impossible for human beings. The metaphor of the child shows that this human impossibility is shattered by God's grace for those who are ready to accept the shocking good news. It also reminds us of what the apostle Paul has clearly seen, namely, that the better righteousness is that which God gives us freely. To children and such as these belongs the Kingdom, without any qualifications, good works or merits. Whoever wants to enter the Kingdom must receive it like children do. This is not the whole gospel of Jesus Christ, but it is the heart of it.

The evangelists' interpretations

We have not received this saying about the Kingdom directly from the lips of Jesus, nor is it for us any longer an unattached "word of the Lord" without any literary context. The four evangelists have not only transmitted this saying to us. By placing it in different contexts within their gospels, they have also interpreted it. In so doing, they were sensitive to the situation and questions of the particular churches for whom they wrote. This has coloured the evangelists' understanding of what Jesus said and influenced the emphasis with which they transmit the word about receiving and entering the Kingdom.

Mark, followed by Luke, transmitted this saying as part of the story on how Jesus received the children (Mark 10 : 13-16). This changes somewhat the meaning of the original story. Now the accent tends to shift in that passage from verse 14 to verse 15. The metaphor of the children begins to overshadow Jesus' attitude to the actual children who were brought to him. Consequently, the first saying of Jesus (v. 14b) must now be differently translated and interpreted than was suggested for the original story. It no longer refers "to these and other such children...", but rather "to people who are like such children..."

Mark transmitted this scene with the two sayings of Jesus as part of a wider literary unit: the passage is preceded by a discussion with Pharisees and disciples on marriage and divorce (Mark 10 : 2-15). It is followed by a discussion with a rich man and with the disciples about earthly possessions and the renunciation of material wealth (Mark 10 : 17-31). These three narratives form together a small catechism about the domestic matters of marriage, children and material possessions. With this arrangement, Mark has given the sayings of Jesus a new context and finality, namely, that of ethical teaching in the congregation.

Two even broader contexts can be discerned. The first one extends from Mark 10 : 1 (the beginning of the way to Judea and to the cross) to Jesus' entry into Jerusalem (Mark 11 : 1-11). In this grouping of narratives, one notices a persistent antithesis between the humble and the exalted, the poor and the rich, the last and the first, the smallest and the greatest, the one who serves and the one who is served, leading up to the climax of Jesus' entry into Jerusalem as the humble, and at the same time exalted, king. The other context is that of the central part of Mark's gospel (Mark 8 : 27-10 : 45), which contains the three announcements of the forthcoming suffering and exaltation of the Son of Man. Placed in wider contexts, these sayings about the children and the Kingdom contribute to the central message of Mark's gospel, namely, that Jesus, the messianic king, has come in quite an unexpected way. He has turned upside down our criteria of judgment. To confess this Jesus as the messianic king, is to imply that we ourselves be changed and be set on the way to the cross.

Matthew has kept the story of Jesus and the children within the same literary framework as Mark, but he made some significant editorial changes. Firstly he omitted the saying about entering the Kingdom (Mark 10 : 15) from this story (Matt. 19 : 13-15), giving it another historical and literary context (Matt. 18 : 3 within Matt. 18 : 1-5; see below chapter four). Secondly, Matthew changed and shortened both the beginning and the end of the story: the attention is concentrated less on those who bring the children and on Jesus' emotions than on the children themselves and the fact that Jesus blessed them. Finally, Matthew completed the catechetical instruction about marriage, children and material possessions by adding a saying about the unmarried state of life (Matt. 19 : 10-12). As elsewhere in his gospel, Matthew shows here a special pedagogical concern. The gospel material is edited and put together in such a way that it becomes a teaching on how to live more righteously than the Scribes and Pharisees. Within the larger framework of Matthew's gospel, this teaching on marriage, celibacy, children and material possessions introduces the fifth section which leads up to the sermon on the Last Judgment (Matt. 24-25).

The saying about entering into the Kingdom in its Matthean context emphasizes objective humility. The first part of this saying: "unless you turn and become like children" (which differs from Mark's and Luke's version) as well as the second part: ". . . you will never enter the Kingdom of Heaven" have already been discussed. The new literary context in which Matthew has placed this saying will be analysed in chapter four. Yet Matthew — and Matthew alone — has added a whole sentence to the words of Jesus: "Whoever humbles himself like this child, he is the greatest in the Kingdom of Heaven" (Matt. 18 : 4), and this addition has still to be examined. While in the preceding sentence Jesus had spoken about the children (plural), here he points to "this child" (singular), referring back to verse 2. This is an indication that, originally, the two sentences did not belong together. The second is a proverbial saying which perhaps went back to an actual statement of Jesus which appears elsewhere in the New Testament: "Whoever exalts himself will be humbled, and whoever humbles himself will be exalted" (Matt. 23 : 12; cf. Luke 14 : 11; 18 : 14; I Peter 5 : 6; James 4 : 10). Matthew has probably combined this unattached wisdom-saying with the words about entering the Kingdom, because it expressed precisely his understanding of what it means to become like a child. The Greek words which are usually translated by "humble", "humility" or "to humble oneself" most often denote in both the Old and the New Testaments not a subjective state of mind, but an objective state of self-abasement and dependency. Whoever wants to enter the Kingdom must stop aspiring to be the greatest in the Kingdom. The disciples must turn around and see how small, dependent and objectively humble a child is. Before God they, too, must experience this state of "smallness". Then they, too, will be called blessed (Matt. 5 : 3-11).

Luke followed Mark exactly with regard to both the place and wording of the saying about receiving and entering the Kingdom (Luke 18 : 15-17). Yet at the beginning of the story, he replaced "children" with "infants" and enhanced the event by adding: "they were *even* bringing infants..." Like Matthew, Luke avoided the reference to Jesus' indignation at the disciples and replaced it with a positive initiative: "Jesus called them to him". Matthew had already shortened the closing verse about Jesus' significant gestures, but Luke totally omitted it, possibly because he considered both the indignation and such intimate gestures of love as being beneath the dignity of the spirit-filled Lord. The closing verse may also have been omitted because Luke wanted to end with the climax of Jesus' saying. This would correspond with Luke's most significant editorial change, namely, the different literary context into which he placed the story.

Here, Jesus' reception of the children is not preceded by the discussion about marriage and divorce like in Mark's and Matthew's gospels. Luke's gentile Christian readers would hardly have understood much of such complicated matters of Jewish law and custom. Moreover, Luke had already summarized this teaching in an earlier chapter (Luke 16 : 18). The context is therefore not a catechetical teaching about domestic matters. The scene where Jesus lets the children come to him immediately follows two parables found only in Luke's gospel, that of the unjust judge (Luke 18 : 1-8) and that of the Pharisee and the tax collector (Luke 18 : 9-14). Luke specified that Jesus told his disciples the first parable "to the effect that they ought always to pray and not lose heart" (v. 1). The second one was told "to some who trusted in themselves that they were righteous and despised others" (v. 9), and the conclusion reads like Matthew's addition to the saying on who could enter the Kingdom: "Every one who exalts himself will be humbled, but he who humbles himself will be exalted" (v. 14). Then follows immediately the scene where the disciples hinder the children from coming to Jesus. This scene, and the two sayings of Jesus which are its climax, serve as an epilogue and conclusion to the two preceding parables. This literary unit forms part of the large middle part of Luke's gospel, the so-called "travel narrative" (Luke 9 : 51-19 : 28). Within this wider context of teaching, the saying in Luke 18 : 17 summarizes well Luke's account of the teaching which Jesus gave to his disciples on the way from Galilee to Jerusalem. Who can become and remain Jesus' disciple? Who can receive the Kingdom? Not people like the self-righteous Pharisee of the parable, but people who wait and pray, people like an infant crying out for help and begging with outstretched empty hands.

4 · A Child in the Midst of Them

Matt. 18:1-5; Mark 9:33-37; Luke 9:46-48

The term most commonly associated with children in the Roman world undoubtedly was *erudire*, a Latin verb with the root *rudis* which means "raw", "unformed", "uninformed". Children were regarded as "raw material" to be shaped and educated. Also, for Jews, children were important and cherished in the first place as schoolchildren, as those to be taught and disciplined. In striking contrast to this whole attitude of his time, Jesus put a child in the midst of his disciples in order to teach them a basic lesson. For him, the child was not raw material for education, but the symbol of true discipleship and, moreover, a true representative of himself and of God. This symbolic act of Jesus and the novelty of his teaching can only be fully appreciated if seen against the background of the ancient Graeco-Roman and Jewish ways of education.

Education in the Graeco-Roman world

The Greeks have rightly been called the people of education. In the course of their ancient history, a rich variety of educational philosophies were developed and translated into practice. All looked back to the great ideal, namely, the world of Homer where from among the young people the elected few had been developed to become heroes of a new generation. Whether in Sparta, Athens or Rome, youth gathered to sing the mighty acts of the Homeric heroes.

Meanwhile, however, military techniques had changed. Wars were no longer won by the exploits of knightly individuals, but by well-disciplined armies of common men who knew how to obey, to endure and to die. This brought about one of the most deliberately planned and ruthlessly executed systems of education in the world, that of ancient Sparta. From the very first day of life onwards, fitness for war was the only criterion for survival (cf. above p. 6). As the slaves far outnumbered the free citizens and did all the work, the free Spartans had just one full-time, life-long activity: to be educated in and for war. During the first seven years, infants were trained by the proverbial Spartan nurses who: "taught them to be contented and happy, not dainty about their food, nor fearful of the dark, nor afraid to be left alone, nor given to contemptible peevishness and whimpering" (Plutarch, *Lycurgus* 16.3). At the age of seven, both boys and girls were taken over by the state and hardened by war games. At the age of twelve, the training was intensified. "Of reading and writing, they learned only enough to serve their turn; all the rest of their training was calculated to make them obey commands well, endure hardships, and conquer in battle" (Plutarch, *Lycurgus* 16.6). Even the education given in the poetry of Homer, in music, dance and gymnastics served only one purpose: to win in battle. For the same reason, boys had to learn to be cunning and to steal, and they underwent severe tests of survival, of organized flogging and savage fighting in mimic battles. An educational system of this kind, which was entirely built on slavery and geared to war, was bound to lead to decay sooner or later.

In Athens, the teachers attempted to make responsible citizens of the *polis*, the city state, from the raw material of their children. But here, culture (not war) was the aim. This meant educating their character and taste: the education of body, mind and imagination. Of course, boys had also to learn a trade and they did so through apprenticeship. But education proper had much more to do with initiation into a particular style of life which Plato described as follows:

> "The education we speak of is training from childhood in goodness, which makes a man eagerly desirous of becoming a perfect citizen, understanding how both to rule and to be ruled righteously... an upbringing which aims only at money-making or physical strength, or even some mental accomplishment devoid of reason and justice, it would term vulgar and illiberal and utterly unworthy of the name 'education' " (*Laws* 644A).

Ideally, the main educational institution should be the home, and in his essay, "On the Education of Children", Plutarch says so. Yet Athenian fathers were much too busy with civic affairs to devote time to their sons, and the mothers remained almost entirely uneducated for, in contrast to Sparta, no schooling was provided for girls. Thus, only boys of free citizens received any formal education in standardized private schools, and these schools often fell short of Plato's ideal.

In ancient Rome, education took place essentially within the family. The aim was to build character, so that the sons and daughters might become fit for their duties to the gods, the state and the family. A Roman child would first be nurtured by his mother. Sons then came under the tutorage of their father, who, during his whole life-time, retained absolute power over his children, even if the sons attained high offices in the government or army, and the daughters respected positions in society. Cato the Elder (died 149 B.C.) was considered to be the ideal father, and Plutarch wrote about him and his son:

> "As soon as the boy showed signs of understanding, his father took him under his own charge and taught him to read, although he had an accomplished slave, Chilo by name, who was a school-teacher, and taught many boys. Still, Cato thought it not right, as he tells us himself, that his son should be scolded by a slave, or have his ears tweaked when he was slow to learn, still less that he should be indebted to his slave for such a priceless thing as education. He was, therefore, himself not only the boy's reading-teacher, but his tutor in law, and his athletic trainer, and he taught his son not merely to hurl the javelin and fight in armour and ride the horse, but also to box, to endure heat and cold, and to swim lustily through the eddies and billows of the Tiber. His history of Rome, as he tells us himself, he wrote out with his own hand and in large characters, that his son might have in his own home an aid to acquaintance with his country's ancient traditions" (*Cato Major* 20).

This was the ideal. In practice things were often quite different. As explained above, Quintilian attempted to reform the Roman educational system in the 1st century A.D.

The educational theories and practices mentioned so far relate to a period several centuries before Christ. In the time of Jesus, the classic models of ancient Athens and ancient Rome were still influential, but two other pedagogies had begun to characterize the schools. On the one hand, latter stoic philosophy tried to promote the growth of an elite of cosmopolitan sages: people who would be able to educate themselves and become free of all human passions. On the other hand, the rhetoricians aimed at teaching an encyclopaedical knowledge, which tended towards a one-sided intellectual training, leading to the "educated" individual who had superficial answers to everything.

The "era of the child" in the Hellenistic world described earlier (cf. above p. 7) was marked by a far-reaching disintegration of families. Therefore, fathers and mothers played a decreasing role in education. Children of slaves and most girls never went to school.

Boys of free citizens were usually handed over to a *paidagogos* — often not a very gifted slave. His main task was to bring the children to school and to keep watch over them with his rod, so that the children would learn. Looking back to the good old days, Tacitus complained at the turn of the 1st to the 2nd century A.D. that eloquence had fallen from her high estate "because of the laziness of our young men, the carelessness of parents, the ignorance of teachers, and the decay of old fashioned virtue".

> "Nowadays. . . our children are handed over at thier birth to some silly little Greek serving-maid, with a male slave, who may be anyone, to help her — quite frequently the most worthless member of the whole establishment, incompetent for any serious service. It is from the foolish tittle-tattle of such persons that the children receive their earliest impressions, while their minds are still pliant and unformed; and there is not a soul in the whole house who cares a jot what he says or does in the presence of his baby master. Yes, and the parents themselves make no effort to train their little ones in goodness and self-control; they grow up in an atmosphere of laxity and pertness in which they come gradually to lose all sense of shame, and all respect both for themselves and for other people. . ." (*Dialogue on Oratory*, 28, 29).

The jeremiad goes on, and in the Greek and Roman literature of that time many similar complaints about irresponsable *paidagogoi* and unqualified teachers can be found.

Regardless of whether the children had such bad parents, tutors and teachers or whether the ideals of a Plato, Cato or Quintilian were achieved, the aim remained always the *erudire*. Whatever "school" among the above-sketched kinds of educational theory was predominant, according to them all the raw material (the child) had to be shaped into a human being capable of functioning within a human society. All pedagogies were anthropocentric. What was to be shaped out of the children's immature state was the ideal human being, be it the hardened soldier, the responsible citizen, the sage who was above all passions, or the pundit who had answers to every question. Children were valued only as potential future products of the art of education.

Education in the Jewish world

The educational aim of Jewish parents and sages was to discipline (*jasar*) the children who were entrusted to them, so that they might become God-fearing members of the Covenant people. While Graeco-

Roman educational theories and practices were essentially anthropo-centric, centred on the human person and state, those of the Jews were strictly theocentric. The God of Abraham, Isaac and Jacob was seen as the one who disciplined and taught his people to walk according to his will, his *Torah*. Human education meant simply to participate in this divine education.

God was not only the primary teacher, but also the primary subject-matter. In the *Talmud*, a story is told of a young progressive rabbi who wanted to study Greek because he felt that he had already mastered the *Torah*. An older rabbi reminded him of the words of Joshua: "This book of the law shall not depart out of your mouth, but you shall meditate on it day and night" (Josh. 1 : 8). He then admonished the young rabbi with the words: "Go then and consider which is the hour which is neither of the day nor of the night, and in it you may study Greek wisdom" (*Menahoth* 99b). Jewish education was, thus, exclusively religious education, or one could perhaps put it another way and say that Jewish religious education embraced the whole of life. This meant that continuous learning was not just confined to children, but that the whole people, young and old, remained a learning community.

As was stated earlier (cf. above p. 9 ff.), children learned by living, praying and working with their parents. This was especially true of the time *before the Babylonian exile*, when the Israelites had no schools. There were exceptions, however. Young princes were given tutors as we know, for instance, from the fact that the seventy sons of Ahab lived with their guardians in Samaria (II Kings 10 : 1-5). Future scribes had to undergo a long training in reading and writing, arithmetic, law, administration and scribal ethics before taking up their duties as local scribes or as the king's scribe. As guardians of the *Torah*, priests and Levites also needed special education in order to supervise the writing of copies of the *Torah*, to teach its precepts authoritatively, to conduct worship in the Temple and to administer its finances. Though prophecy was not a skill to be learned, nor the prerogative of certain families, prophets nevertheless gathered bands of disciples around themselves where in a religious community the prophetic tradition was taught and transmitted. By far the majority of Israelites, however, passed through no other educational institution than that of the family and its participation in the life, wars and celebrations of the Covenant people.

Children learned the discipline of the *Torah* and the fear and love of the Lord simply through a kind of osmosis, a process of becoming accustomed to it. They came to know God by helping their parents in the work of agriculture and cattle breeding, because this daily work was intimately related to the *Torah*:

> "If you will obey my commandments which I command you this day, to love the Lord your God, and to serve him with all your heart and with all your soul, He will give the rain for your land in its season, the early rain and the later rain, that you may gather in your grain and your wine and your oil. And He will give grass in your fields for your cattle, and you shall eat and be full" (Deut. 11 : 13-15).

Intimately linked with agriculture were the three great religious celebrations (cf. Ex. 23 : 14-17; Deut. 16 : 1-17; Lev. 23 : 4-44). In April, the Passover marked the beginning of the barley harvest and it commemorated at the same time the liberation from slavery in Egypt. Pentecost was celebrated at the beginning of June when the wheat was harvested and this feast also became a memorial of the giving of the *Torah* on Mount Sinai. The festival of tabernacles at the end of September marked the end of the grape harvest and commemorated the journey through the desert to the promised land. Each of these celebrations included many symbolic rites, which recalled the history of salvation and incited the curiosity and questions of all those who did not know the meaning of these rites, especially the children. In the case of the Passover, fathers were actually ordered to answer such questions and thereby teach their children. "You shall tell your son on that day, 'It is because of what the Lord did for me when I came out of Egypt' " (Ex. 13 : 8). Later, this didactic dialogue became part of the Passover ritual and it has remained so until today. The *Mishna* tract on the Passover celebration prescribes the following in connection with the second cup:

> "Here the son asks his father (and if the son has not enough understanding, his father instructs him), 'Why is this night different from other nights? For on other nights we eat seasoned food once, but this night twice; on other nights we eat leavened or unleavened bread, but this night all is unleavened; on other nights we eat flesh roasted, stewed, or cooked, but this night all is roasted'. And according to the understanding of the son, his father instructs him. He begins with the disgrace and ends with the glory; and he expounds from: 'A wandering Aramean was my father...' (Deut. 26 : 5 ff.) until he finishes the whole section" (*Pesahim* 10, 4).

Such questioning and answering must have gone on not only during the three great festivals, but throughout the year, and on such special occasions as the celebration of Sabbath Year or Covenant renewals. The land itself, with its evocative names and monuments, led to teaching. Thus, even the stones erected at the place where the Covenant was renewed under Joshua's leadership had such pedagogical significance. "When your children ask their fathers in time to come, 'What do these stones mean?' then you shall let your children know: 'Israel passed over this Jordan on dry ground... so that all the peoples of the earth may know that the hand of the Lord is mighty; that you may fear the Lord your God for ever' " (Josh. 4 : 21 ff.). Fathers were not only the home-priests, but also the home-catechists and in the book of Deuteronomy particularly, again and again, they are exhorted to tell the story. In the *Shema*, the central affirmation of Jewish faith (Deut. 6 : 4-9; 11 : 13-21; Num. 15 : 37-41), which every believing Jew has to recite daily in the morning and evening, the explicit order to teach with words and symbols is included twice:

> "These words which I command you this day shall be upon your heart; and you shall teach them diligently to your children, and shall talk of them when you sit in your house, and when you walk by the way, and when you lie down, and when you rise. And you shall bind them as a sign upon your hand, and they shall be as frontlets between your eyes. And you shall write them on the doorposts of your house..." (Deut. 6 : 6 ff.; 11 : 18 ff.).

As soon as a child could speak it had to learn by heart the first phrase of the *Shema* and the sentence: "Moses commanded us a law, as a possession for the assembly of Jacob" (Deut. 33 : 4). According to the Deuteronomic legislation, every seventh year the whole people, "men, women, and the little ones" had to be assembled for the public reading of the *Torah*, so "that they may hear and learn to fear the Lord your God, and be careful to do all the words of this law, and that their children, who have not known it, may hear and learn to fear the Lord" (Deut. 31 : 10-13).

All these pre-exilic prescriptions made the Jewish home a continuous, theocentric educational institution. This was still so in the time of Jesus. But, in the 1st century before and after Christ, another educational institution gained significance: the school. It was called *Beth-Sepher*, literally translated: "the house of the Book". It is still not known exactly when these schools were established. According to Josephus, the Mosaic law already "orders that they (that is, the children) shall be taught to read, and shall learn both the laws and the deeds of their forefathers, in order that they may imitate the latter, and, being grounded in the former, may neither transgress nor have any excuse for being ignorant of them" (*Against Apion*, II, 204). It was a Jewish tendency to trace all their institutions back to Moses, and Josephus has simply followed that custom here. As a matter of fact, schools are mentioned for the first time in a short notice in the *Talmud*, according to which Simeon ben Shetah, the brother-in-law of king Alexander Yannai (ca. 100 B.C.), prescribed that children should go to elementary school. In the time of Jesus, many Jews, in fact, knew how to read.

The first more extensive reference to the establishment of elementary schools dates only from the time of Joshua ben Gamla, who was high priest in Jerusalem at about 63-65 A.D. The *Talmud* says of him:

> "Rabbi Judah said in the name of Rab (ca. 200 A.D.): 'Verily Rabbi Joshua ben Gamla should be remembered for good, for had it not been for him the *Torah* would have been forgotten in Israel. For at first, the boy who had a father was taught *Torah* by him, while the boy who had no father did not learn. Later, they appointed teachers of boys in Jerusalem, and the boys who had fathers were brought by them (to the teachers) and were taught; those who had no fathers were still not brought. So then they ordered that teachers should be appointed in every district, and they brought to them lads of the age of sixteen or seventeen. And when a teacher was cross with any of the lads, the lad would kick at him and run away. So then Rabbi Joshua ben Gamla ordered that teachers should be appointed in every district and in every city and that the boys should be sent to them at the age of six or seven years' " (*Baba Bathra* 21a).

It is quite clear why sooner or later schools had to be established. The publication of the book of Deuteronomy in 622 B.C. had already introduced a written code into the life of the Jewish people. During and after the Babylonian exile, much more of the oral teaching was codified, especially by Ezra. The Jews thus became the people of the Book. Local synagogues began to function as the main centres of learning in addition to the Temple, and the scribes gradually replaced the priests and Levites as the main teachers. Moreover, the sayings of the sages, which originally had been collected primarily for the education of princes and scribes, now became handbooks for general education. To the books of Proverbs and Ecclesiastes were added such other wisdom sayings as those of Jesus Sirach and the book of the

Wisdom of Solomon. In the course of the 1st and 2nd centuries B.C., some of the synagogues must have established regular teaching of the *Torah* and the wisdom. A passage in the Jerusalem *Talmud* indicates that, before its destruction, "there were 480 synagogues in Jerusalem, each of which had a Bible school (*Beth-Sepher*) for the study of the Bible and a *Talmud* school (*Beth Talmud*) for the study of the *Mishna*" (*Megillah* 3 : 1, 73d). The first book which the children had to read and study in these elementary schools was the book of Leviticus, a most unlikely first reader!

These schools did not replace the home. Particularly for young children and for daughters, the mother continued to act as the principal teacher. Nor were the educational duties of the father lessened in any way. He had "to instruct his son in the Law, to bring him into wedlock, and to teach him a handicraft" (*Kiddushin* 30b). Indeed, "whoever does not teach his son a trade teaches him to become a robber" (*Tosefta Kiddushin* 1,11). For, as Rabbi Eleazar ben Azariah (ca. 130 A.D.) said according to the *Mishna:* "If there is no meal, there is no study of the Law; if there is no study of the Law there is no meal" (*Aboth* 3, 18).

This intimate relationship between daily work and the study of the Law created the demand for a more thorough teaching of the *Torah* than that which could be given at home. Therefore, more and more, the teachers came to be as honoured as the parents. According to a tract of the *Mishna*, they were even to be given preeminence: "In the study of the Law, if the son gained much wisdom (while he sat) before his teacher, his teacher comes even before his father, since both he and his father are bound to honour the teacher" (*Kerithoth* 6, 9). The *Talmud* goes a step further: "If a man teaches the son of his fellow-student the *Torah*, the Scripture accounts it to him as if he had created him." Rabbi Elazar (3rd or 4th century A.D.) says: "as if he had created the Law itself" (*Sanhedrin* 99b).

On the other hand, children became important because they were *schoolchildren* (cf. above p. 11). The ultimate praise found in the *Talmud* is the following: " 'Touch not mine anointed, and do my prophets no harm' (I Chron. 16 : 22). The former are the school-children; the latter, rabbis. 'The world', said Resh Lakish, in the name of Rabbi Judah Nesiah (ca. 210 A.D.), 'stands only upon the breath of the schoolchildren... Let not the children be kept back from school, even to help in building of the Temple' " (*Shabbat* 119b).

The reversal of teaching

During the time of Jesus, both in the Graeco-Roman and the Jewish world, teaching was one-way: from the adults towards the children. Whether the raw material present in a child had to be formed into a fully human being or whether a small immature member of the Covenant people had to be disciplined by the knowledge and fear of the Lord, in both cases it was the child which was at the receiving end and which had importance only as a potential learner.

It is in the context of such Graeco-Roman and Jewish concepts of education that the incident reported in Mark 9 : 33-37, Luke 9 : 46-48 and Matthew 18 : 1-5 must be considered. In all three accounts, the occasion of Jesus' actions and words is the disciples' question about who among them was the greatest. In Jesus' response, a child becomes central, not as the one who receives instruction, but as the one whose very presence becomes the clue to answering the disciples' question. Consequently, a reversal in the teaching/learning situation occurs, which indicates at the same time a reversal of being: the first must be last; the least one is great, the person who humbles him- or herself like a child is the greatest in the Kingdom of Heaven.

This general message is common to all three accounts. Yet a detailed study reveals many differences in the context and the wording, as well as significant additions and omissions. Each evangelist has recorded and interpreted in his own way the events and words which he received from the oral tradition of the Church. Through this tradition, the Church knew of Jesus' response to the disciples' question about who is the greatest. It also knew of the occasion when Jesus put a child in the midst of the disciples in order to teach them a lesson. Whether these two memories of incidents which occurred during the earthly life of Jesus originally referred to one and the same event can no longer be ascertained. Mark seems to combine two different incidents (Mark 9 : 33-35 and 9 : 36-37), which can be read and understood separately from one another. Luke's and Matthew's accounts clearly report the disciples' question and the incident with the child as two parts of the same event. A comparison of the three parallel texts reveals the particular emphasis of each evangelist (cf. Worksheet IV in Appendix D).

Mark has put the passage at the beginning of a collection of sayings and incidents which are only loosely related to one another: Jesus' teaching about true greatness (Mark 9 : 33-37), the episode of the strange exorcist (9 : 38-40), the saying about the cup of water

(9 : 41), the warnings concerning temptations (9 : 42-48) and the sayings about fire and salt (9 : 49-50). All these conversations and sayings involve teaching for the disciples who, despite the repeated forewarning of the Passion, did not understand Jesus' way. This teaching was given in the intimacy of "the house" (v. 33). There are linguistic indications supporting the idea that already in the oral tradition these passages were transmitted together: special "link-words" relate the different parts and thus facilitate committing them to memory (cf. for example: "in my name" in v. 37, "in your name" in v. 38 and again "in my name" in v. 41; "one of these little ones" in v. 42 recalls "the child" in v. 37; the "fire" links v. 48 with v. 49 and the "salt" makes the link between v. 49, v. 50a, b and v. 50c). Such link words may also have held together the two parts of vv. 33-35 and vv. 36-37, because in Aramaic the term *talya'* means both "servant" and "child".

Mark started the teaching about true greatness twice; first in a typically Markan, anecdotal way (vv. 33-34 which are perhaps meant to introduce the whole sequence of teaching up to v. 50), and then again in verse 35a, where Jesus sits down to teach and calls the twelve to him. It is Jesus who takes the initiative, both in asking what the disciples had discussed on the way and in responding to their argument despite their silence. Only Mark reported Jesus' saying about the first and the last (v. 35b) as an immediate response to the disciples' query. In the parallel accounts, Matthew omitted this saying and Luke put a similar wording at the very end of the passage (Luke 9 : 48b).

The teaching about the first and the last is a saying in the style of the Proverbs. Variations of it occur in the gospels no less than seven times. Opposed to one another are the following notions:

first — last of all and servant of all:	in Mark 9 : 35
great — your servant:	in Mark 10 : 43; Matt. 20 : 26
first — (your) slave (for all):	in Mark 10 : 44; Matt. 20 : 27
greatest — your servant:	in Matt. 23 : 11
least among you — great:	in Luke 9 : 48
greatest — the youngest:	in Luke 22 : 26
leader — one who serves:	in Luke 22 : 26

All these versions point to an unexpected reversal. In Mark 9 : 35b, this saying stops short and answers the query of the disciples about true greatness.

Following the first teaching, Mark immediately added a second one: that concerning the reception given to a child. With a didactic gesture Jesus first enacts part of his message by putting a child in the midst of the disciples and taking the child in his arms (v. 36). Then comes the amazing message itself: "Whoever receives one such child in my name receives me; and whoever receives me, receives not me but him who sent me" (v. 37). The child becomes, here, the fully representative symbol of Jesus and of God. The significance of this astonishing representative quality of a child will be discussed more fully later. Before that, it is necessary to examine in which context Luke and Matthew have set this saying about the child, and how they changed Mark's wording in the light of their own testimony to Jesus.

Luke has radically shortened the sequence of teachings. Of Mark's eighteen verses, only five remain. After the second announcement of the Passion comes briefly the teaching about true greatness (Luke 9 : 46-48) and the conversation about the strange exorcist (9 : 49-50). Then begins Luke's long account of Jesus' travel from Galilee to Jerusalem (9 : 51-19 : 27). It is probably for this reason that, contrary to Mark's version, the above sequence of teaching is no longer placed in Capernaum. Jesus and his disciples are, according to Luke's understanding, already on the border between Galilee and Samaria (cf. vv. 51 ff.). Consequently the teaching is no longer reported as a private instruction for the twelve "in the house".

The disciples argued and wondered in their minds who was the greatest among them. They did so, not in an outward discussion as Mark reported, but inwardly in "the thought of their hearts". As elsewhere in Luke's gospel, Jesus then shows a miraculous knowledge of their secret thoughts (v. 47a). He challenges them by putting a child, not in the midst of them, but by his side (v. 47b). This is immediately followed by the saying about the significance of receiving this child (v. 48a, b). Contrary to Mark, Luke's wording does not speak of the general: "one of such children" (Greek text of Mark 9 : 37a), but puts it more concretely: "this child", referring back to the particular child at Jesus' side. Only then did Luke add the saying about the least and the great (Luke 9 : 48c). With such an arrangement of the material, the total passage becomes an integrated whole. The incident with the child is now clearly part of Jesus' answer to the disciples' question. The word "great" at the end of the last verse concludes the query about "the greatest" in the first verse.

What is the main emphasis in Luke's version? The accent does not lie on the necessary humility and servanthood of Christian believers, as is the case in the first part of Mark's account (Mark 9 : 33-35) and in Matthew's parallel (especially Matt. 18 : 4). Elsewhere in his gospel (cf. Luke 22 : 24-27), Luke also reported Jesus' call for humility. Here, however, the answer to the question of true greatness is different. It is to be seen in Jesus' gesture of setting a child at his very side. In this case, the child symbolizes "the smallest among all of you" (v. 42c). As will be shown, in Luke's gospel this expression refers in the first place to the poor in the congregation. Jesus receives exactly these smallest ones, gives them the place of honour and thereby true greatness. To receive "this child" and the smallest disciples whom it symbolizes, to do so "in Jesus' name" by seeing them in their special relationship with Jesus — this is the true quest for greatness.

Matthew has integrated part of the Markan sequence of teaching into the "discourse on the Church", which comprises the whole of his eighteenth chapter and which concludes the fourth part of his gospel (Matt. 13 : 53-18 : 35). This discourse clearly falls into two sequences. The first begins with the teaching about true greatness (Matt. 18 : 1-5), follows Mark with the warnings about temptations (vv. 4-9) and leads up to the parable of the lost sheep (vv. 10-14). The second sequence starts with the teaching on how to deal with sin in the Christian community (vv. 15-18), adds sayings about prayer and forgiveness (vv. 19-22), and again concludes with a parable, the one about the unforgiving servant (vv. 23-35).

It is in this context that Matthew's rendering of the teaching on true greatness must be interpreted. In a truly rabbinic fashion, the passage begins with the disciples — no more the twelve — addressing a question to their master. This question concerns not simply the greatest in general but: "Who is the greatest in the Kingdom of Heaven?" In Matthew's gospel, the Kingdom often includes the present life of the Christian community on earth, which will lead to its fullness in the coming heavenly Kingdom. It has, therefore, a strongly ethical connotation. How should Christians live here and now? In answer to this question, Jesus puts a child in the midst of the disciples. Contrary to Mark's and Luke's account, Jesus begins by "calling to him" a child. This expression serves elsewhere in the gospels as a stereotype introduction for gathering those who will be taught by Jesus. Yet, here, it is not the child who is to be instructed, but the disciples. The child becomes the lesson. According to Matthew's account, Jesus does not take this child in his arms or put the child by his side. Neither the child's relationship to Jesus nor the receiving of such a child are emphasized. Here, the child figures as an example of humility. It is for this reason that Matthew — and he alone — has placed Jesus' saying about becoming like a child (vv. 3-4) into the context of the teaching about true greatness. This particular saying, also Matthew's own interpretation, has already been examined in the last chapter.

The story could have ended with verse 4, and the saying about the receiving of children could have been omitted. Yet Matthew had too great a respect for the gospel material which he received from the tradition, be it from Mark's gospel or by oral transmission. He therefore added a shortened version of the saying (Matt. 18 : 5; cf. Mark 9 : 37). However, in Matthew's gospel, this saying no longer forms an integral part of the teaching on true greatness. It has become the introduction of the next teaching: "Whoever receives one such child in my name receives me; but whoever causes one of these little ones who believe in me to sin, it would be better..." (vv. 5 ff.). Several translations of the Bible make a paragraph in between verses 4 and 5. Indeed, this corresponds better to the structure of the text than having a paragraph between verses 5 and 6.

The shift from descriptive to metaphorical language is important. In verse 2, the term "child" refers to an actual child who is being put in the midst of the disciples as a visual lesson for objective humility. The "child" in verse 5 has a different function: it symbolizes "these little ones". "These", as the next verses show, are none other than the weak members of the Christian community.

Children as metaphors of the Church

The examination of the teaching on true greatness as understood and interpreted by the evangelists showed a shift from the real child to the metaphor of the child which symbolizes the Church. In Mark, the shift remains implicit only. In Luke, "this child" is later assimilated with the "least among the disciples". In Matthew, a parallel between "such a child" and "these little ones" is established. This shift must now be examined in greater detail.

According to Matthew's testimony in particular, Jesus had a great concern and love for these "little ones". Who are they? Not the children. It is true that a child can become the metaphoric symbol for the "little ones". It would be wrong, however, to apply all sayings about the "little ones", the poor, the humble or the babes to actual children. Sometimes, the "little ones" are a designation of the whole membership of the Church. Mark's version of the warning not to cause "one of these little ones who believe in me to sin" (Mark 9 : 42) can possibly be understood in this way. The context into which Matthew has placed this same saying suggests a more restricted group. Here, "the little ones" are not the believers in general, but a special category of Christians, namely, particularly vulnerable believers, those who tend to become "lost sheep" (cf. Matt. 18 : 10-14). In Luke's gospel in particular, "the little ones" are identified with the poor. "Fear not, little flock, for it is your Father's good pleasure to give you the Kingdom" (Luke 12 : 32). This encouragement from Jesus, which is reported only by Luke, probably refers not to the small number of believers, but to economic vulnerability (cf. the immediately preceding anxiety about food and clothing in Luke 12 : 22-31). Using a vulnerable, seemingly unimportant and often despised child as a symbol for the weak and poor members of the Church is singularly appropriate. As the child is to be received and surrounded by special care and love, so these "little ones" are to be given special consideration in the Church.

There is still another category of Christians who, like children, are to be received with special care and respect and who are also called "little ones". It is significant that Matthew has placed the saying about the cup of water (cf. Mark 9 : 41) at the end of Jesus' missionary exhortation (Matt. 10 : 42). Matthew's expanded version of this saying about the cup begins with a sentence which recalls Jesus' words about the receiving of a child: "He who receives you receives me, and he who receives me receives him who sent me" (Matt. 10 : 40). The "you" are the disciples sent out as witnesses. They stand in the line of the prophets and the righteous (v. 41). The passage concludes with the saying about the cup of water: "And whoever gives to one of these little ones even a cup of cold water because he is a disciple, truly, I say to you, he shall not lose his reward" (v. 42). Matthew has introduced here the theme of "the little ones" in a saying which according to Mark was addressed to the disciples in general (Mark 9 : 41). Do "the little ones" refer here, generally, to the early Christian missionaries? Or did Matthew want to single out a special category of missionaries, namely, those who had no special gifts for this task, but nevertheless announced the gospel "in weakness and in much fear and trembling" as Paul once wrote about his own missionary ministry in Corinth (I Cor. 2 : 1 ff.)?

No matter how this question is answered, "the little ones" designate here vulnerable early Christian missionaries who suffered, were persecuted and despised because of their witness to Christ. It may be that in Mark 9 : 33-42 this special meaning is also implied.

A similar group of people are probably referred to in the parable of the Last Judgment (Matt. 25 : 31-46), although it must be acknowledged that the interpretation of this parable remains problematic and controversial. There, Christ the king says to those who had fed, clothed and visited people in need: "Truly, I say to you, as you did it to one of the least of these my brethren, you did it to me" (Matt. 25 : 40, 45). Probably these people in need are not generally the poor, but specifically "the little ones", namely persecuted Christian witnesses. Here, Jesus' solidarity with these least of his brethren is paralleled to his solidarity with children.

The metaphor of the child can be overemphasized. Already Mark, Matthew and Luke seem to have been more interested in what a child symbolizes than in Jesus' attitude to actual children. This is even more true for the remainder of the New Testament. For instance, the apostle Paul wrote profound meditations about our adoption as God's children, but when it came to real boys and girls, his attitude remained exactly that of a Jew of his time, apparently unaffected by Jesus' extraordinary words and actions concerning children. Therefore, it is all the more important to emphasize, once more, the amazing way in which Jesus identified himself with a child.

The hidden presence in the child

When Jesus took a child and put it in the midst of the disciples or at his own side, He said that with this child He himself and even God was present. We have acknowledged that this child then became a metaphor for the disciples and for special groups within the early Church. However, this does not alter the fact that, originally, Jesus must have spoken about that real child which He had just taken into his arms. What message is contained in his action and words?

First of all, Jesus commends the children to our loving care. Whether he spoke of children in general or referred especially to children of the poor and to orphans is not specified. In the New Testament, the expression "to receive somebody" always includes hospitality, be it as a temporary guest or through adoption as a permanent member of the family. Such hospitality for children and adoption were common practice in the Jewish environment of Jesus.

Both the precepts of the *Torah* and the exhortations of the prophets contain clear calls to be just and charitable to orphans because God himself is their defender (Ex. 22 : 22 ff.; Isa. 1 : 23).

Stories such as that of the infant Moses who was adopted by the daughter of Pharaoh (Ex. 2 : 5 ff.) and of the orphaned Esther who had been adopted by Mordecai (Esther 2 : 7) were often retold. "Be like a father to orphans", wrote the wisdom teacher, Jesus Sirach (4 : 10), and the sayings of the rabbis after him include similar exhortations. Rabbi Jose said: "Why does God love widows and orphans? Because their eyes are turned upon him, as it is said, 'A father of the fatherless and a judge of the widows' (Ps. 68 : 5). Therefore, anyone who robs them is as if he robbed God, their Father in heaven" (*Exodus Rabbah*, *Mishpatim* 30,8).

And the *Talmud* ordains: "Scripture counts to someone who has educated an orphan boy or girl in his house as if he had begotten such children" (*Megillah* 13a). Similarly, the sectarian Jewish movement of the Essenes used to receive orphans into their community as Josephus reports: "Marriage, they disdain, but they adopt other men's children, while yet pliable and docile, and regard them as their kin and mould them in accordance with their own principles" (*War* II, 120).

In the rabbinic sayings about the receiving of orphaned children, great emphasis is laid on the reward of such charitable acts. The adoption of children by the Essenes served at least in part to promote the continuation of their community. In the saying of Jesus, another emphasis is made. All three evangelists report that Jesus said: "Whoever receives one such child 'in my name' ". Behind this formula lies a Semitic expression which, in the gospels, is often better rendered with "for my sake" or "for my name's sake" (cf. Mark 8 : 35; 10 : 29; 13 : 9). It points to a relationship. Children are to be hospitably received because of Jesus' special relationship with them, because they are his special representatives.

According to Jewish thinking, "the envoy of the king is as the king himself" (*Baba Kamma* 113b). That the envoy and representative of Jesus should be a child must have been as shocking and incomprehensible to the disciples as the announcement that the Messiah had to suffer. No reasonable human explanation could be given for the children's special relationship to God's Kingdom (Mark 10 : 14). Moreover, there are no obvious human explanations for the children's special relationship with Jesus. However, for those steeped in biblical thinking, this identification of Jesus with children once again confirms the special kind of love which is in the heart of the biblical God:

> "It was not because you were more in number than any other people that the Lord set his love upon you and chose you, for you were the fewest of all peoples; but it is because the Lord loves you" (Deut. 7 : 7-8).
>
> "When Israel was a child, I loved him, and out of Egypt I called my son... I took them up in my arms; but they did not know that I healed them. I led them with cords of compassion, with the bands of love, and I became to them as one who eases the yoke on their jaws, and I bent down to them and fed them" (Hos. 11 : 1-4).
>
> "Thus says the Lord God to Jerusalem: Your origin and your birth are of the land of the Canaanites; your father was an Amorite, and your mother a Hittite. And as for your birth, on the day you were born your navel string was not cut, nor were you washed with water to cleanse you, nor rubbed with salt, nor swathed with bands. No eye pitied you, to do any of these things to you out of compassion for you; but you were cast out on the open field, for you were abhorred, on the day that you were born. And when I passed by you, and saw you weltering in your blood, I said to you in your blood, 'Live, and grow up like a plant of the field'. And you grew up and became tall and arrived at full maidenhood; your breasts were formed, and your hair had grown; yet you were naked and bare. When I passed by you again and looked upon you, behold, you were at the age for love; and I spread my skirt over you, and covered your nakedness: yea, I plighted my troth to you and entered into a covenant with you, says the Lord God, and you became mine" (Ezek. 16 : 3-8).

"Whoever receives me, receives (not me but) him who sent me." In the *Talmud* a similar statement is made: "The one who receives the scribes is like one who receives the *Shechinah*" (*Berakhoth* 64a). That scribes and rabbis whose whole life was devoted to the study of the *Torah* were related to the *Shechinah*, the visible manifestation of God's presence, can be understood within the Jewish context. As school-children, that means in so far as they were taught the *Torah* and disciplined by it, even children had a special relationship to the *Shechinah* (cf. the saying in *Lamentation Rabbah* 1,33, quoted above pp. 27 ff.). Yet here it is the relationship with Jesus which makes these children representatives of God. As such, they are our teachers. In their objective humility and need, they cry "mother", "father", "Abba", and they stretch out their empty hands. If we want to learn how to receive the Kingdom and how to become God's representatives, we must learn it from the child in our midst.

Appendix A · New Testament Terms for the Child

In the New Testament, one finds no less than thirteen different Greek words for designating a child in the broad sense of the term. The following is a list of these terms (in the order of the Greek alphabet) with the meaning they had in classical Greek and the Greek commonly spoken in New Testament times:

brephos: "young", "fruit of the body", that is: *(a)* an already conceived, but as yet unborn child or animal; *(b)* a "baby", a new born child or animal.

thēlazōn: participle of the verb *thelazo:* "one who sucks", "suckling".

thygatēr: (a) "daughter", of no specific age, but indicating a female descendant; *(b)* in the New Testament, also, more generally "offspring", "inhabitants of a place".

thygatrion: diminutive of *thygatēr*, indicating a "little daughter" or "young daughter".

korasion: "little girl", the diminutive of *kora:* "girl", a common Greek term which does not appear in the New Testament.

nēpios: a term which functions both as an adjective and a noun with different shades of meaning: *(a)* somebody who is "simple", "ignorant" or "foolish"; *(b)* somebody who is still "immature", "young" or in a figurative sense "childish"; *(c)* "infant", "immature child".

paidarion: diminutive of *pais: (a)* a "little child", boy or girl, who can walk and is beginning to talk; *(b)* a "lad", "youngster", in this case almost synonymous with *neanias* and *neaniskos*, that is, a "young man"; *(c)* a "young slave".

paidion: diminutive of *pais: (a)* a "small child" who is still under the supervision of its mother or nurse, that is, up to the age of 7; *(b)* later more generally a "child", boy of girl, of any age.

paidiskē: female diminutive of *pais:* (a) "young girl" or "young woman"; (b) "maid", "slave-girl".

pais: derived from the root for "small", "little": (a) usually a "boy", but occasionally also a "girl", sometimes referring to the age-group of 7-14, sometimes irrespective of age; (b) "descendant", be it a son, a son-in-law, a daughter or a young animal; (c) familiar vocative for those who are younger in age, sometimes "pupil", "disciple"; (d) a "male servant", "slave".

teknion: so far not found in the literature outside the New Testament: "little child", used as a vocative of endearment.

teknon: literally, "what has been begotten or born", designating (a) a "child" seen under the aspect of its origin, be it a boy, a girl or the young of an animal; (b) sometimes used as the vocative for familiar address, irrespective of age; (c) in the New Testament the plural is mainly used for "descendants", "progeny", "people".

hyos: the male counterpart to *thygatēr*. It designates: (a) the "son", irrespective of age; contrary to *pais* and its derivatives, the term does not evoke a little boy, but it emphasizes the physical or spiritual descent and special affiliation of a person; (b) more generally, "descendant", "offspring", "heir"; (c) vocative for a beloved follower; (d) especially if used with a genitive case: one who shares a special relationship with or likeness to somebody or something.

The word statistics on p. 56 show that in the New Testament these terms are used with a vastly different frequency. An inventory of the passages where they occur leads to the following observations with regard to the theme of Jesus and the children.

1. Terms of origin, belonging or social status

Most of the New Testament passages where one of the terms listed above is used do not refer to children as such. "Children", "sons", "daughters" and even "little children" usually specify the origin and the belonging of those addressed, rather than their age.

This is particularly true for the term which occurs the most frequently: *hyos*. It translates the Hebrew term: *ben* (in Aramaic *bar*) which in the Hebrew Old Testament is used some 4,850 times. There it (a) designates physical descendants and relatives, (b) functions as a broader term of association or (c) points to a relationship with God. The same four shades of meaning are found in the New Testament:

1) Jesus is called the "Son of Mary" (Matt. 1 : 21-25; Luke 1 : 31; 2 : 7),

the "Son of Joseph" (Matt. 1 : 16; Luke 3 : 23), the "Son of David" (Matt. 1 : 1). Similarly, Joseph is called "Son of David" (Matt. 1 : 20) and many other texts refer to this physical descent (Matt. 7 : 9; 17 : 15; 20 : 20 ff.; Luke 15 : 1 ff.).

2) Students of the Pharisees can be called "sons of the Pharisees" (Matt. 12 : 27; Acts 23 : 6). Mark's association with the apostle is expressed with "my son Mark" (I Peter 5 : 13). Similarly, such expressions as "your son" and "sons of Abraham" designate not only physical descent, but an association created "through grace" (see John 19 : 26; Luke 19 : 9; Gal. 3 : 7).

3) Often a positive or negative relationship is indicated with such terms as "sons of the Kingdom" (Matt. 8 : 12), "of peace" (Luke 10 : 6), "of light" (John 12 : 36), "of the resurrection" (Luke 20 : 36), but also "sons of the devil" (Acts 13 : 10) or "sons of perdition" (John 17 : 12).

4) The relationship to God is indicated with the expression "sons of God" (Matt. 5 : 9; Rom. 8 : 14), "sons of your Father who is in heaven" (Matt. 5 : 45), "sons of the Most High" (Luke 6 : 35) etc.

The term *thygatēr* occurs much more rarely in both the Old and the New Testaments. This is because the words *ben/bar/hyos* often include women, and one must remember the prevalence of masculine bias in the ancient Near East and the Hellenistic world. Of the 28 New Testament passages containing *thygatēr*, 19 refer to direct physical descent (see Matt. 9 : 18; 10 : 35; 14 : 6) and four to broader origins and associations, for example; "daughters of Aaron" (Luke 1 : 5) or "daughters of Jerusalem" (Luke 23 : 28). Only in Matt. 9 : 22 is a relational significance used when Jesus addressed the woman suffering from hemorrhage with the words: "Take heart, daughter". Similarly, once only, in II Cor. 6 : 18, is the term "daughter" used for designating the special relationship with God. Except for the daughter of "about twelve years of age" in Luke 8 : 42, and possibly the daughter of Herodias, all other "daughters" are grown up women, among them Anna who "was of great age" (Luke 2 : 26).

Moreover, terms which designate little children are frequently used in the New Testament as indications of origin and belonging or as familiar vocatives for adults. Thus, *teknon* refers to a new-born child in Rev. 12 : 4 ff. and in I Thess. 2 : 7, it is used for children taken care of by a nurse. In most of the 99 occurrences, however, this term has similar shades of meaning as *hyos*. It designates the physical descent, irrespective of age (for example: Matt. 10 : 21; 15 : 26; 21 : 29; Luke 15 : 31; Matt. 3 : 9; John 8 : 39), it refers to a particular good or bad relationship: "children of the flesh" or "children of God" in Rom. 9 : 8, or it is a term of endearment to loved ones as in I Cor. 4 : 14; I Tim. 1 : 2, etc. The diminutive *teknion* is exclusively used as a vocative for adults (see John 13 : 33 as well as seven occurrences in I John). Although the term *pais* originally referred to smallness and is, in fact, used for little children in Acts 20 : 12, it also designates a *neanias*, a young man. Similarly, *paidion* is not only used for actual children, but is used three times as a direct designation for Jesus' disciples (John 21 : 5; I John 2 : 14, 18) and occasionally as an allusion to the disciples (Matt. 18 : 5; Heb. 2 : 13, cf. Isa. 8 : 16 ff.).

Some of the terms designate the social status of a person. For example, the word *paidiskē* is used 13 times in all in the New Testament. However the accent is not on the fact that these are young girls or women, but on the fact that they function as servants. Thus, the maid who challenged Peter in the courtyard of the high priest had to watch the door (John 18 : 17), the slave-girl with the spirit of divination had to bring profit to her owners (Acts 16 : 16), and Hagar is mentioned by Paul because she was a slave (Gal. 4 : 22-31). Similarly, more than half of the occurrences of the term *pais* emphasize servanthood. They designate either actual servants and slaves (for example: Matt. 8 : 6 ff.; 14 : 2; Luke 12 : 45), they speak about David or Israel as the servant of God (Luke 1 : 54, 69; Acts 4 : 25), or as will presently be shown, they refer to Jesus as "God's servant".

It is important to note that, in the New Testament, actual children are never called "children of God". We see that already in the Old Testament the Hebrew term *yeled*, which designates an actual child, is never used in this way. The people of Israel or their king can be called a child *(ben/bar)* of God. Similarly, in the New Testament, Christians are called God's children; but in these cases, the term *hyos* or more frequently *teknon* are used, and never *paidion* or other designations for small children. Children are not romantically divinized in the Bible.

2. Titles given to Jesus

Five times Jesus is called God's *pais*, the *Servant of God*. Once, in Matt. 12 : 18, this title explicitly refers back to a servant song in II Isaiah (Isa. 42 : 1). In the four other passages (Acts 3 : 13, 26; 4 : 27, 30), the title is used in apostolic proclamation and prayer.

Throughout the New Testament, Jesus is confessed to be *hyos theou*, the *Son of God*. Famous synoptic texts are Mark 1 : 11; 9 : 7; 14 : 61; 15 : 39 and Peter's confession according to Matt. 16 : 16. John uses this title in such key texts as John 1 : 34, 49; 3 : 18; 5 : 25; 11 : 4; 17 : 1. While this title never occurs in the pastoral letters, in I Peter and only relatively seldom in Acts, Hebrews and Revelation, it is used 16 times in Paul's letters (for example: Rom. 1 : 3 ff.; 8 : 3, 29, 32; Gal. 2 : 20; 4 : 4, 6; I Thess. 1 : 10) and no less than 14 times in I John (see: 1 : 3, 7; 3 : 8; 4 : 9, 15; 5 : 9-12).

Less frequently, Jesus is called: *ho hyos*, the *Son*. This happens, for instance, in Matt. 11 : 27; 24 : 36; 28 : 19. The title often occurs in John's gospel, for example: John 3 : 16 ff., 35 ff.; 5 : 19-26; 6 : 40; 8 : 35 ff., but only once in Paul's letters (I Cor. 15 : 28). This title is frequently used again in Hebrews (for example: 1 : 2; 3 : 6; 5 : 8) and in the letters of John (see: I John 2 : 22-24).

Jesus is seldom called the *Son of David*, and most passages containing the term are found in Matthew's gospel: Matt. 1 : 1; 9 : 27; 15 : 22; 20 : 31 ff. and parallels; 12 : 23; 21 : 9, 15; 22 : 42, 45 and parallels.

Occurring much more often is the enigmatic title: *Son of Man*. With a few exceptions (Acts 7 : 56, Heb. 2 : 6; Rev. 1 : 13), this expression is found only in the four gospels, and always in sayings of Jesus. These sayings can be grouped into four categories. *(a)* The words of the necessary suffering of the Son of Man; (for example: Mark 8 : 31; 9 : 31; 10 : 33 ff.).

WORD STATISTICS *

	Matt.	Mark	Luke	John	Acts	Paul's Letters	Pastoral Letters	Heb.	Catholic Letters	Rev.	Total NT	Greek OT
brephos	—	—	5	—	1	—	1	—	1	—	8	5
thēlazōn	1	—	—	—	—	—	—	—	—	—	1	ca 10
thygatēr	8	5	9	1	3	1	—	1	—	—	28	ca 400
thygatrion	—	2	—	—	—	—	—	—	—	—	2	—
korasion	3	5	—	—	—	—	—	—	—	—	8	ca 25
nēpios	2	—	1	—	—	10	—	1	—	—	14	ca 50
paidarion	—	—	—	1	—	—	—	—	—	—	1	ca 150
paidion	18	12	13	3	—	1	—	3	2	—	52	ca 100
paidiskē	1	2	2	1	2	5	—	—	—	—	13	ca 50
pais	8	—	9	1	6	—	—	—	—	—	24	ca 300
teknion	—	—	—	1	—	—	—	—	7	—	8	—
teknon	14	9	14	3	5	29	10	—	12	3	99	ca 200
hyos	89	34	77	55	21	40	—	24	27	8	375	ca 3000

* Adapted from Robert MORGENTHALER, *Statistik des neutestamentlichen Wortschatzes*, Zürich/Frankfurt: Gotthelf-Verlag, 1958.

(b) The ministry of the Son of Man on earth; (see: Mark 2: 10, 28; Matt. 8 : 20; 11 : 18 ff.; Luke 11 : 30; Mark 10 : 45). *(c)* The words of the coming Son of Man; (for example: Mark 8: 38; 13: 26; 14: 62). *(d)* Typical Johannine Son of Man sayings are, for example: 1 : 51; 3 : 13 ff.; 5 : 27; 12 : 23.

The fact that Jesus is confessed to be God's Servant, his Son, *the* Son *par excellence*, as well as the fact that He is recognized in the various ministries of the Son of Man, might possibly throw new light on Jesus' attitude to children. However, this question cannot be pursued within the framework of this study, because it would require detailed discussion of the highly complex meanings of the titles mentioned. Only in one of the texts examined in this book does a title, the "Son of Man", occur: in Matt. 11 : 19; Luke 7 : 34. Here, as in Mark 2 : 10 and Matt. 8 : 20, "Son of Man" probably equals "man"; Jesus must, in this case, have used the expression in order to emphasize his humanity. Neither in this passage nor elsewhere does there seem to be a direct relationship between the *pais* and *hyos* titles and the theme of this book.

3. Various age levels and Jesus as a child

In the New Testament, there is no exact delimitation between the various age groups. The only distinctions made are those between fathers and children (Eph. 6 : 4), between the mature and the immature (I Cor. 13 : 11; 14 : 20) or between the older and the younger (I Tim. 5 : 1 ff.). The exhortations in I John 2 : 12 ff. seem to be addressed alternately to little children, children, young men and fathers. But, in fact, they probably envisage only fathers and young men. The *paidia* in v. 14a stand parallel to the *teknia* in v. 12a. Like the *paidia* in v. 18a and the *teknia* throughout the letter, "children" is a term used as a familiar vocative for all Christians addressed by the apostle.

Among the words designating actual children, some terms are given preference when speaking about infants, while others refer more often to older children, although no clear-cut distinction is made. In a quotation from Ps. 8, the *thelazōn*, the "suckling", appears together with the *nēpios* (Matt. 21 : 16), which in this passage must be translated with "babe". The *brephos* either designates the "babe in the womb" (Luke 1 : 41, 44), the new born infant (Luke 2 : 12, 16; Acts 7 : 19 and in a figurative way I Peter 2 : 2) or the little child and early childhood (Luke 18 : 15; II Tim. 3 : 15).

All other terms cover a wider range of age groups. Thus, *paidion* can be used for a new-born infant (John 16 : 21), for the infant Moses (Heb. 11 : 23), the infant John the Baptist (Luke 1 : 59, 66, 76, 80), or the infant Jesus (frequently in Matt. 2 and Luke 2). The same term probably designates children of various ages in such passages as Matt. 11 : 16; 14 : 21; 18 : 2; 19 : 3; Mark 7 : 28 and Luke 11 : 7. In the healing of the daughter of Jairus, the *paidion* (Mark 5 : 39 ff.) is called both a *thygatrion* (v. 23) and a *korasion*

(vv. 41 ff.; so also in the parallel text of Matt. 9 : 24 ff.), and it is specified that she was 12 years old (v. 42). In the only other occurrence of *thygatrion* (Mark 7 : 25), no specification of age is given. The same is true of the other three times when *korasion* is used (Matt. 14 : 11; Mark 6 : 22, 28), designating the little daughter of Herodias.

An even wider range of age groups is included in the term *pais*. When the word does not refer to the social status and the servant function, but to age, it can designate little boys up to two years of age (Matt. 2 : 16), the 12-year old boy Jesus (Luke 2 : 43), the 12-year old daughter of Jairus (Luke 8 : 51) and boys of unspecified age (Matt. 17 : 18; 21 : 15; John 4 : 51). But the unfortunate Eutychus, the person who fell out of a window during a very long sermon given by Paul, is also called a *pais* (Acts 20 : 12), although he was already a young man (*neanias*, v. 9). The only passage with *paidarion* (John 6 : 9) does not specify the age. It probably refers to a "youngster", but may also indicate the social rank: "a young slave".

For the purposes of this study, it must be underlined that no less than 13 times Jesus himself is called an infant or a child: twice a *brephos* (Luke 2 : 12, 16), 10 times a *paidion* (Matt. 2 : 8, 9, 11, 13, 14, 20, 21; Luke 2 : 17, 27, 40) and once a *pais* (Luke 2 : 43). Jesus knew existentially something of the vulnerability and objective humility of a child. It is also noteworthy that the canonical gospels do not depict the child Jesus as a boy with miraculous power. This stands in striking contrast both to the Hellenistic descriptions of child heroes and to the later apocryphal childhood gospels. Nevertheless, it is true that when the 12-year old boy Jesus remained in the temple, "all who heard him were amazed at his understanding and his answers" (Luke 2 : 47). This verse has been the point of departure for many miraculous stories about Jesus as a child. It must be remembered, however, that the point of the whole narrative in Luke 2 : 41-52 does not come in v. 47, but in v. 49. The narrative concludes the childhood stories whose main emphasis throughout Luke 1 and 2 is the manifestation of God's glory in Jesus when He enters his place, the temple of Jerusalem.

4. The children and the *nēpioi*

The children *(paides)* who shouted "hosanna" in the temple courtyard are compared to the *nēpioi* in Ps. 8 : 2 (Matt. 21 : 16). The comparison with Luke 19 : 37, 39 might suggest that these "children" were in fact disciples. It is more likely, however, that Matthew wanted to refer to actual children, and *nēpios* does not here have the overtones of immaturity or childishness.

The seven passages where the term *nēpios* occurs in the New Testament letters also evoke childhood, but with quite different nuances. Paul once used the verb "to be or act like a *nēpios*": "Brethren, do not be children *(paidia)* in your thinking; be babes *(nēpiazein)* in evil, but in thinking be mature" (I Cor. 14 : 20). Here *paidia* has a pejorative sense, being opposed to maturity, while *nēpiazein* receives a relatively positive significance. It would be wrong to translate it with "innocent" in the sense of an innate purity. Rather, it refers to the fact that a small child does not yet have the corrupting experience of the world's wickedness. This is the only passage in the New Testament letters where a *nēpios* acts, in a particular sense, as a model.

All other passages use the term with overtones of deficiency, immaturity, instability, or foolishness. The main accent no longer lies on the tender age of the child, but on the imperfect state of the *nēpioi*, whatever their age, which must be overcome. In Rom. 2 : 20, Paul described the "outward Jew" who claims to be a "corrector of the foolish, a teacher of the *nēpioi*". The foolish and the *nēpioi* are thus put together. Paul himself had to become such a teacher of *nēpioi*, because he could not address the Christians in Corinth "as spiritual men, but as men of the flesh, as *nēpioi* in Christ" (I Cor. 3 : 1). A similar judgment is made in Heb. 5 : 13 which refers to Christians who cannot be given solid food, but live on milk only because they are still *nēpioi*. (In I Peter 2 : 2, the same image is used in a non-pejorative way, yet there the term *nēpios* is avoided!) This lack of growth in the Christian life manifests itself also in the great instability of the *nēpioi* who, according to Eph. 4 : 14, are "tossed to and fro and carried about with every wind of doctrine".

A more juridical significance of the term *nēpios* predominates in Gal. 4 : 1 and 3. Here the time of immaturity, when the heir is still a *nēpios*, is contrasted with the fullness of time, when through Christ's mission an adoption *(hyothesia)* becomes possible. This great change has already occurred, and Christians must therefore no longer remain under the *paidagogos* of the law (Gal. 3 : 24). Yet, at the same time, Paul still waits expectantly for the time of final revelation and perfection. In the context of this hope, he again used the *nēpios* as an example, this time emphasizing the aspect of imperfection and limitation: "When I was a *nēpios*, I spoke like a *nēpios*, I though like a *nēpios*, I reasoned like a *nēpios*; when I became a man, I gave up what belongs to a *nēpios*" (I Cor. 13 : 11).

The passages containing the word *nēpios* in the New Testament letters are essentially for the purposes of ethical exhortation and are oriented towards education. The famous saying of Jesus in Matt. 11 : 25 ff.; Luke 10 : 21 ff. has quite another orientation. There, Jesus thanks God "that thou hast hidden these things from the wise and understanding and revealed them to *nēpioi*; Yea, Father, for such was your gracious will". Who are the *nēpioi* in this passage? They are not contrasted against adults, but "the wise and understanding". These undoubtedly referred to the religious elite who understood the wisdom of the *Torah*. In the Syriac Apocalypse of Baruch, written in Palestine at the same time as the gospels of Matthew and Luke, the following exhortation is found: "Prepare your hearts, that you may obey the law, and be subject to those who in fear are wise and understanding; and prepare your souls that you may not depart from them" (2 Bar. 46 : 5).

Jesus' thanksgiving is in marked opposition to this exhortation. Not to the wise and understanding has God given true insight into the mystery of the Kingdom, namely, all that was happening through Jesus (cf. Matt. 4 : 11 ff.); it pleased God to reveal this to the *nēpioi*. Most scholars agree that, in this context, it is not children who are designated here, and they connect these *nēpioi* with different groups. Some see in them the "poor in spirit", mentioned in Matt. 5 : 3, who are the descendants of the Old Testament *anawim*, the "poor of Yahweh". Others think more of the "poor of the land" (the *am ha-aretz*) who were despised by the religious authorities and turned to Jesus for release from their heavy yoke forced upon them by scribes and Pharisees and by the landowners (cf. Matt. 11 : 28-30). Still others identify the *nēpioi* in this saying of Jesus with the "little ones", with all the various shades of meaning of this term (cf. above pp. 47 ff.). It is impossible to distinguish clearly between these various groups. Jesus may have alluded to several or all of them. Paradoxically, the one New Testament story where *nēpios* alludes least to actual children (namely, Matt. 11 : 25 ff.; Luke 10 : 21 ff.) is the one which stands theologically nearest to the sayings and actions of Jesus with regard to the children.

Appendix B · Annotated Bibliography

During the last two decades, only relatively few exegetical studies on Jesus and the children have been published. The commentaries on Mark's, Matthew's and Luke's gospels deal, of course, with the relevant passages. But, as far as I could discover, none of them devotes a special excursus to this theme. Many biblical word books include articles on the child. Especially informative are the following contributions to the *Theological Dictionary of the New Testament*, edited by **G. Kittel** and **G. Friedrich**, Grand Rapids, Wm. B. Eerdmans, 1964-1976: G. Bertram, *"nēpios, nēpiazein"*, in Vol. IV, pp. 912-923; A. Oepke, *"pais, paidion, paidarion, teknon, teknion, brephos"*, in Vol. V, pp. 636-654; P. W. von Martitz, G. Fohrer, E. Schweizer, E. Lohse, W. Schneemelcher, *"hyos, hyothesia"*, in Vol. VIII, pp. 334-399.

By far the most thorough but not the most easily readable study remains the one by **S. Legasse**, *Jésus et l'Enfant: "enfants", "petits" et "simples" dans la tradition synoptique*, Paris, Editions Gabalda, 1969, 375 pp. After the introduction, the author first makes a literary examination of Mark 9 : 33-37; Luke 9 : 46-48; Matt. 18 : 1-5, of Mark 10 : 13-16; Luke 18 : 15-17; Matt. 19 : 13-15 and of Matt. 21 : 14-16 (pp. 17-50). In the second and third chapters, the concern expressed in the gospels for the "little ones" *(mikroi)* and the "simple ones" *(nēpioi)* is examined. In this connection, such passages as Matt. 18 : 6, 10; Matt. 18 : 12-14; Matt. 10 : 42; Matt. 25 : 31-46; Mark 9 : 36-37; Luke 12 : 32 and Matt. 11 : 25-30; Luke 10 : 21-22 are discussed (pp. 51-185). The fourth and fifth chapters are devoted to the relationship between the child and the Kingdom according to Mark and Luke and to the figure of the child in Matthew's gospel (pp. 187-268). The last part of Legasse's study deals with the status of the child in the Greek and Jewish milieu of the New Testament, the parable of the children playing in the market place (Matt. 11 : 16-19; Luke 7 : 31-35) and with the historic Jesus' attitude to the children (chapters VI-VIII, pp. 269-336). The book ends with some general conclusions. S. Legasse has summarized the main results of this volume in the article on "L'En-

fant dans l'Evangile", in *La Vie Spirituelle*, No. 570, 1970, pp. 409-421.*
With regard to studies dealing with individual passages on Jesus and the children, the following proved to be most helpful: **F. Mussner**, "Der nicht erkannte Kairos (Matt. 11: 16-19; Luke 7: 31-35)", in *Biblica*, Vol. 40, 1959, pp. 599-612, makes a careful analysis of the parable of the children's game. An attempt to relate exegesis with present-day application is made in the fifth chapter of **H. Stock**, *Studien zur Auslegung der synoptischen Evangelien im Unterricht*, Gütersloh, Bertelsmann, 1959, "V. Die Gotteskindschaft: Jesus und die Kinder, Markus 10: 13-16 und Matthäus 18: 1-5/Par." (pp. 175-201). Exegetically, this study is based on the interpretation of the texts by German scholars such as M. Dibelius, R. Bultmann and E. Lohmeyer. Its special merits are the implications drawn from exegesis for religious education lessons adapted to various age groups.

A similar link between exegesis and the search for contemporary meaning is made in a book devoted to the so-called "children's gospel" (Mark 10: 13-16), edited by **G. Krause**, *Die Kinder im Evangelium*, Stuttgart/Göttingen, Klotz Verlag, 1973. First, G. Klein analyses Mark 10: 13-16 from a literary, redaction-history and tradition-history point of view, drawing conclusions for the proclamation of this passage in today's world (pp. 12-30).

The second contribution is by I. Ludolphy, "Zur Geschichte der Auslegung des Evangelium infantium". She shows that, despite the early liturgical and pastoral use of Mark 10: 13 ff. in relation to children's baptism, only the polemic against the Anabaptists at the time of the Reformation led to the use of this text as an exegetical justification for children's baptism. She then examines how this text is situated in recent studies on children's baptism (pp. 31-51).

The third contribution deals with the iconographic history of Mark 10: 13-16, written by B. and B. Diebner, "Beispiele zur Bildgeschichte des sogenannten 'Kinder-Evangeliums'" (with nine reproductions). The development from the earliest known artistic representation (ca. 800 A.D.) to present-day art work shows how Jesus' attitude to children was quite differently understood in the different centuries (pp. 52-78).

Finally, the editor G. Krause writes on "Jesus der Kinderfreund: Reflektionen und Meditationen zum heutigen Verständnis". In the light of the modern rediscovery of the child (J. J. Rousseau, C. Dickens, F. M. Dostojewski, E. Key, R. M. Rilke and contemporary authors) Mark 10: 13 ff. is re-examined and its message for today is explored (pp. 79-112).

An article by **J. I. H. McDonald** on "Receiving and Entering the

---

* For a narrative exegesis of the texts on Jesus and the children, see *A Child? A Story for Adults* by Hans-Ruedi Weber; Redhill, National Christian Education Council, 1979. A cassette recording of this story is also available from the National Christian Education Council.

Kingdom: A Study of Mark 10 : 15", in *Studia Evangelica*, Vol. VI, 1973, pp. 328-332, is helpful because of its extensive use of rabbinic parallels. Also, **J. Jeremias'** discussion of Mark 10 : 13 ff. in his *Infant Baptism in the First Four Centuries*, London, SCM Press, 1960, pp. 48-55, contains interesting rabbinic and patristic references.

The passage on the teaching about true greatness (Mark 9 : 33-37 and parallels) is analysed by **A. Descamps**, "Du discours de Marc IX, 33-50 aux paroles de Jésus", in *La Formation des Evangiles*, Louvain, Desclée de Brouwer, 1957, pp. 152-177. The author first shows how probably already in the period of the oral tradition miscellaneous sayings of Jesus were gathered together in the so-called "discourse on community" with the help of recurring key words and link words. He then examines the content of the actual sayings of Jesus which lay behind this discourse.

The intriguing parallels to the synoptic texts on Jesus and the children in the gospel of Thomas are discussed in the article by **H. C. Kee**, " 'Becoming a Child' in the Gospel of Thomas", in *Journal of Biblical Literature*, Vol. 82, 1963, pp. 307-314. The author comes to the conclusion that relevant logia 4, 21, 22, 37 and 46 do not contain additional sayings of the earthly Jesus, but "that the synoptic themes have been placed by the Gospel of Thomas in service of a view point that is anthropologically, eschatologically, and theologically alien to the New Testament" (p. 313).

Surveys of the relevant biblical passages concerning the children are given in many biblical-theological lexicons and encyclopaedias. A good summarizing article is the one by **A. Goettmann**, "L'attitude fondamentale du disciple: l'enfance spirituelle", in *Bible et Vie Chrétienne*, Vol. 77, October 1967, pp. 32-45.

The article by **A. Oepke** on *"pais"*, etc., mentioned earlier, gives a good survey of the position of children in the ancient Graeco-Roman and Jewish worlds. See further **J. Leipoldt**, "Vom Kinde in der alten Welt", in *Reich Gottes und Wirklichkeit:* Festgabe für A. Dedo Müller, Berlin, Evang. Verlagsanstalt, 1961, pp. 343-351, and **H. Herter**, "Das unschuldige Kind", in *Jahrbuch für Antike und Christentum*, Vol. IV, 1961, Münster, Aschendorff, 1962, pp. 146-162.

There are many detailed studies about the education of children in the ancient world. The most readable monograph on this subject is the one by **W. Barclay**, *Educational Ideals in the Ancient World*, London, Collins, 1959. The author describes the education among the Jews, the Spartans, the Athenians and the Romans. After an examination of the Christian attitude to pagan culture, the closing chapter deals with "The Child in the Early Church" (pp. 234-262). A comparable study is that by **W. Jentsch**, *Urchristliches Erziehungsdenken: Die Paideia Kyriu im Rahmen der hellenistisch-jüdischen Umwelt*, Gütersloh, Bertelsmann, 1951. The emphasis in this study is laid on the linguistic analysis of the Greek and Hebrew verbs for education *(paideuein, jasar)* and on the examination of early Christian educational theories on the background of Graeco-Roman and Jewish educational philosophies. In this connection, the author also discusses the subject of the child in the New Testament (pp. 205-216). A more limited subject within the same field is dealt with by **H. Mueller**, *A Critical Analysis of the Jewish Educational Philosophy in Relationship to the Epistles of St. Paul*, St. Augustin, Steyler Verlag, 1967, and in the article on "Education" by **A. Demsky** and **Y. Moriel** in the *Encyclopaedia Judaica*, Vol. VI, Jerusalem, Keter Publishing House, 1971, pp. 382-403.

Appendix C · Graeco-Roman and Jewish Texts on Children and Education

To be or not to be

Should a new-born infant be kept alive or not? This was the first question raised in the Graeco-Roman world whenever a child was born. Not everywhere had this decision about life and death become as institutionalized as in Sparta (cf. Plutarch's information in *Lycurgus* 16.1 ff., quoted on p. 6), but child exposure was common practice (cf. above pp. 6 ff.), and great philosophers defended it. Plato (4th century B.C.) prescribed for his ideal state:

> "The offspring of the good, I suppose, they will take to the pen or crèche, to certain nurses who live apart in a quarter of the city, but the offspring of the inferior, and any of those of the other sort who are born defective, they will properly dispose of in secret, so that no one will know what has become of them" (*Republic* 460 C).

The fact that children were disposable in this way led to depopulation. The Greek historian, Polybius (2nd century B.C.) described the situation of his country as follows:

> "In our own time, the whole of Greece has been subject to a low birth rate and a general decrease of the population, owing to which cities have become deserted and the land has ceased to yield fruit, although there have neither been continuous wars nor epidemics. If, then, anyone had advised us to send and ask the gods about this, and find out what we ought to say or do, to increase in number and make our cities more populous, would it not seem absurd, the cause of the evil being evident and the remedy being in our own hands? For as men had fallen into such a state of pretentiousness, avarice, and indolence that they did not wish to marry, or if they married to rear the children born to them, or at most as a rule but one or two of them, so as to leave these in affluence and bring them up to waste their substance, the evil rapidly and insensibly grew. For in cases where of one or two children the one was carried off by war and the other by sickness, it is evident that the houses must have been left unoccupied, and as in the case of swarms of bees, so by small

degrees cities became resourceless and feeble. About this it was of no use at all to ask the gods to suggest a means of deliverance from such an evil. For any ordinary man will tell you that the most effectual cure had to be men's own action, in either striving after other objects, or if not, in passing laws making it compulsory to rear children" (*Histories* XXXVI, 17.5-10).

Jews saw in the birth of a child, especially of a boy, a great blessing (cf. above pp. 8 ff.). The God of Abraham, Isaac and Jacob was recognized as the one who takes pity on an exposed child (Ezek. 16 : 5 ff.). Child exposure was therefore abhorred (cf. the information of Tacitus, *History* 5.5, quoted on p. 9). Similarly, the early Christian writers severely condemned such a disregard for a new-born child. Thus, Justin Martyr (middle 2nd century A.D.) wrote:

"As for us, we have been taught that to expose newly-born children is the part of wicked men; and this we have been taught lest we should do anyone an injury, and lest we should sin against God; first, because we see that almost all so exposed (not only the girls, but also the males) are brought up to prostitution... And anyone who uses such persons, besides the godless and infamous and impure, intercourse may possibly be having intercourse with his own child, or relative, or brother" (*First Apology* 27).

Educational ideals of Greeks and Romans

In the Graeco-Roman world, children were first of all seen as those to be educated (cf. above pp. 34 ff.). It must be added immediately that education was mainly concentrated upon boys, and that only the free born were considered at all.

The treatise on *The Education of Children*, which is probably wrongly attributed to Plutarch (ca. 100 A.D.), begins characteristically with the sentence: "Let us consider what may be said of the education of free-born children". Children of slaves never appear in this treatise, and the author acknowledges that his suggestions may be applicable for the education of the rich only and not for poor children of the common people. Yet he considers this to be "a minor matter" (*Education* 11 E, F).

A short description of educational aims and practices in Sparta, Athens and Rome is given above on pp. 34 ff. The main purpose was to shape the raw material (children) into useful adult persons and citizens. Thus, Lucian (2nd century A.D.) described the educational ideal of Athens' law-giver, Solon, in the following way:

"We have not thought it sufficient for each man to be as he was born, either in body or in soul, but we want education and disciplines for them by which their good traits may be much improved and their bad altered for the better. We take example from the farmers, who shelter and enclose their plants while they are small and young, so that they may not be injured by the breezes: but when the stalk at last begins to thicken, they prune away the excessive growth and expose them to the winds to be shaken and tossed, in that way making them more fruitful" (*Anacharsis* 20).

While Lucian used the work of farmers as a parable for the art of education, Plato compared the same process to the taming of an animal:

"Just as no sheep or other grazing beast ought to exist without a herdsman, so children cannot live without a tutor, nor slaves without a master. And, of all wild creatures, the child is the most intractable; for in so far as it, above all others, possesses a fount of reason that is as yet uncurbed, it is a treacherous, sly and most insolent creature. Wherefore the child must be strapped up, as it were, with many bridles — first, when he leaves the care of nurse and mother, with tutors, to guide his childish ignorance, and after that with teachers of all sorts of subjects and lessons, treating him as becomes a free born child. On the other hand, he must be treated as a slave; and any free man that meets him shall punish both the child himself and his tutor or teacher, if any of them does wrong" (*Laws* 808 D.E.).

Sometimes, children did not survive such "taming". According to Lucian, Solon prepared Anacharsis for what he would see in Sparta:

"Above all, do not laugh if you see them (that is, Spartan children) getting flogged at the altar and dripping blood while their fathers and mothers stand by and are so far from being distressed by what is going on that they actually threaten to punish them if they should not bear up under the stripes, and beseech them to endure the pain as long as possible and to be staunch under the torture. As a matter of fact, many have died in the competition, not deigning to give in before them the eyes of their kinsmen while they still had life in them, or even to move a muscle of their bodies; you will see honours paid to their statues, which have been set up at public cost by the state of Sparta. When you see all that, do not suppose them crazy, and do not say that they are undergoing misery without any stringent reason, since it is due neither to a tyrant's violence nor to an enemy's maltreatment. Lycurgus, their law-giver, could defend it by telling you many good reasons which he has discerned for punishing them; he is not unfriendly to them, and does not do it out of hatred, nor is he wantonly wasting the young blood of the city, but he desires that those who are destined to preserve their country should be tremendously staunch and superior to every fear. Yet, even if Lycurgus does not say so, you see for yourself, I suppose, that such a man, on being captured in war, would never betray any Spartan secret under torture inflicted by the enemy, but would laugh at them and take his whipping, matching himself against his flogger to see which would give in" (*Anacharsis* 38).

It would be wrong to consider Spartan education as the ideal of the whole Graeco-Roman world. Plato's definition of education (*Laws* 644 A; quoted on p. 35) and Plutarch's description of Cato as an ideal father (*Cato Major* 20; quoted on p. 36) complement the picture. In the first century A.D., there were also pedagogues who, like Quintillian (cf. above p. 7), emphasized that:

"pupils will require some relaxation, not merely because there is nothing in this world that can stand continued strain, and even unthinking and inanimate objects aie unable to maintain their strength unless given intervals of rest, but because study depends on the good will of the student, a quality that cannot be secured by compulsion. Consequently, if restored and refreshed by a holiday they will bring greater energy to their learning and approach their work with greater spirit of a kind that will not submit to be driven. I approve of play in the young; it is a sign of a lively disposition... There are, moreover, certain games which have an educational value for boys... I disapprove of flogging, although it is the regular custom... Children are helpless and easily victimized, and... therefore no one should be given unlimited power over them" (*Institutio* I, 3.8-11, 13, 17).

Education was seen as a life-long and many-sided art which Plato described for Athens as follows:

"They teach and admonish them from earliest childhood till the last day of their lives. As soon as one of them grasps what is said to him, the nurse, the mother, the tutor, and the father himself strive hard that the child may excel, and as each act and word occurs they teach and impress upon him that this is just, and that unjust, one thing noble, another base, one holy, another unholy, and that he is to do this, and not do that. If he readily obeys, — so; but if not, they treat him as a bent and twisted piece of wood and straighten him with threats and blows. After this, they send them to school and charge the master to take far more pains over their children's good behaviour than over their letters and harp playing. The masters take pains accordingly, and the children, when they have learnt their letters and are getting to understand the written word as before they did only the spoken, are furnished with works of good poets to read as they sit in class, and are made to learn them off by heart. Here they meet with many admonitions, many descriptions and praises and eulogies of good men in times past, that the boy in envy may imitate them and yearn to become even as they. Then, also, the music-masters in a similar sort take pains for their self-restraint, and see that their young charges do not go wrong: moreover, when they learn to play the harp, they are taught the works of another set of good poets, the song makers, while the master accompanies them on the harp; and they insist on familiarizing the boys' souls with the rhythms and scales, that they may gain in gentleness, and by advancing in rhythmic and harmonic grace may be efficient in speech and action; for the whole of man's life requires the graces of rhythm and harmony. Again, over and above all this, people send their sons to a trainer, that having improved their bodies they may perform the orders of their minds, which are now in fit condition, and that they may not be forced by bodily faults to play the coward in wars and other duties. This is what people do, who are most able; and the most able are the wealthiest. Their sons begin school at the earliest age, and are freed from it at the latest. And when they are released from their schooling, the city next compels them to learn the laws and to live according to them as after a pattern, that their conduct may not be swayed by their own light fancies, but just as writing masters first draw letters in faint outline with the pen for their less advanced pupils, and then give them the copy book and make them write according to the guidance of their lines, so the city sketches out for them the laws devised by good law-givers of yore, and constrains them to govern and be governed according to these" (*Protagoras* 325C-326D).

Educational ideals of the Jews

Among the Jews, also, education was a life-long discipline, although for them everything was centred on their God and his *Torah* (cf. above pp. 37 ff.). Children had to be disciplined to behave according to the *Torah* and thereby to become holy. Thus, the scribe, Jesus Sirach (ca. 200 B.C.), described education as follows:

"He who loves his son will whip him often, in order that he may rejoice at the way he turns out.

He who disciplines his son will profit by him, and will boast of him among acquaintances.

He who teaches his son will make his enemies envious, and will glory in him in the presence of friends.

The father may die, and yet he is not dead, for he has left behind him one like himself; while alive he saw and rejoiced, and when he died he was not grieved; he has left behind him an avenger against his enemies, and one to repay the kindness of his friends.

He who spoils his son will bind up his wounds, and his feelings will be troubled at every cry.

A horse that is untamed turns out to be stubborn, and a son unrestrained turns out to be wilful.

Pamper a child, and he will frighten you; play with him, and he will give you grief.

Do not laugh with him, lest you have sorrow with him, and in the
end you will gnash your teeth.

Give him no authority in his youth, and do not ignore his errors.
Bow down his neck in his youth, and beat his sides while he is young,
lest he become stubborn and disobey you, and you have sorrow of
soul from him.

Discipline your son and take pains with him, that you may not be
offended by his shamelessness" (*Sirach* 30 : 1-13).

This rather grim picture of disciplining must be complemented by
rabbinic sayings on education quoted above on pp. 11 ff. and 42 ff. The
Jewish historian, Josephus (ca. 100 A.D.), saw in the educational system
a particular characteristic of his people:

"Above all, we pride ourselves on the education of our children,
and regard as the most essential task in life the observance of our
laws and of the pious practices, based thereupon, which we have
inherited" (*Against Apion* I.60).

"Religion governs all our actions and occupations and speech; none
of these things did our law-giver leave unexamined or indeterminate.

"All schemes of education and moral training fall into two categories;
instruction is imparted in the one case by precept, in the other by
practical exercising of the character. All other legislators, differing
in their opinions, selected the particular method which each preferred
and neglected the other. Thus, the Lacedaemonians and Cretans
employed practical, not verbal, training; whereas the Athenians and
nearly all the rest of the Greeks made laws enjoining what actions
might or might not be performed but neglected to familiarize the
people with them by putting them into practice.

"Our legislator, on the other hand, took great care to combine both
systems. He did not leave practical training in morals inarticulate;
nor did he permit the letter of the law to remain inoperative. Starting
from the very beginning with the food of which we partake from
infancy and the private life of the home, he left nothing, however
insignificant, to the discretion and caprice of the individual. What
meats a man should abstain from, and what he may enjoy; with
what persons he should associate; what period should be devoted
respectively to strenuous labour and to rest — for all this our
leader made the Law the standard and rule, that we might live under
it as under a father and master, and be guilty of no sin through
wilfulness or ignorance. For ignorance, he left no pretext. He
appointed the Law to be the most excellent and necessary form of
instruction, ordaining, not that it should be heard once for all
or twice or on several occasions, but that every week men should

desert their other occupations and assemble to listen to the Law and to obtain a thorough and accurate knowledge of it, a practice which all other legislators seem to have neglected" (*Against Apion* II. 171-175).

From early childhood to maturity

Should free-born children be nursed by their mothers and educated by their parents or should they be handed over to nurses, tutors and teachers? In the Graeco-Roman world, opinion was divided on this subject. In the Spartan system of education, as well as according to Plato's ideal state, children were reared outside their homes. Yet, as mentioned earlier, Cato took the education of his son into his own hand (cf. p. 36), and in Plutarch's treatise on education the following is suggested:

"Mothers ought, I should say, themselves to feed their infants and nurse them themselves. For they will feed them with a livelier affection and greater care, as loving them inwardly, and, according to the proverb, to their finger tips. But the goodwill of foster mothers and nursemaids is insincere and forced, since they love for pay "(*Education* 3C).

Similarly, Tacitus wrote about ancient Rome:

"In the good old days, every man's son, born in wedlock, was brought up not in the chamber of some hireling nurse, but in his mother's lap and at her knee. And that mother could have no higher praise than that she managed the house and gave herself to her children" (*Dialogue on Oratory* 28).

The fact that the situation was no longer like this in Tacitus' own time (ca. 100 A.D.) has already been reported (cf. p. 37). Also, Plutarch complained:

"Nowadays, the common practice of many persons is more than ridiculous; for some of their trustworthy slaves they appoint to manage their farms, others they make masters of their ships, others their factors, others they make house stewards, and some even money lenders; but any slave whom they find to be a wine bibber and a glutton, and useless for any kind of business, to him they bring their sons and put them in his charge.

"Nowadays there are some fathers who deserve utter contempt, who, before examining those who are going to teach, either because of ignorance, or sometimes because of inexperience, hand over their children to untried and untrustworthy men. And this is not so ridiculous if their action is due to inexperience, but there is another case which is absurd to the last degree. What is this? Why, sometimes even with knowledge and with information from others who tell them of the inexperience and even of the depravity of certain teachers, they nevertheless entrust their children to them; some yield to the flatteries of those who would please them, and there are those who do it as a favour to insistent friends.

"Heaven help us! Does a man who bears the name of father think more of gratifying those who ask favours than he thinks of the education of his children?" (*Education* 4A-E).

As in all times, there must have been good and bad parents, tutors and teachers, in the same way as there has always existed the picture of a good or bad school boy. Here is the description of a good school boy's day in a treatise (wrongly) attributed to Lucian:

"He rises at dawn from his unwed couch, washes away with pure water such sleep as still remains in his eyes and after securing his shirt and his mantle with pins at the shoulder 'he leaves his afther's hearth with eyes bent down' and without facing the gaze of anyone he meets. He is followed by an orderly company of attendants and tutors, who grip in their hands the revered instruments of virtue, not the points of a toothed comb that can caress the hair nor mirrors that without artists' aid reproduce the shapes confronting them, but behind him come many-leaved writing tablets or books that preserve the merit of ancient deeds, along with a tuneful lyre, should he have to go to a music master.

"But, after he has toiled zealously through all the lessons that teach the soul philosophy, and his intellect has had its fill of these benefits of a standard education, he perfects his body with noble exercises. For he interests himself in Thessalian horses. Soon, after he has broken in his youth as one does a colt, he practises in peace the pursuits of war, throwing javelins and hurling spears with unerring aim. Next come the glistening wrestling schools, where beneath the heat of the midday sun his developing body is covered in dust; then comes the sweat, that pours forth from his toils in the contest, and next a quick bath and a sober meal suited to the activities that soon follow. For again he has his school masters, and records of deeds of old with hints for the study of such questions as what hero was brave, who is cited for his wisdom, or what men cherished justice and temperance. Such are the virtues which he uses to irrigate his soul while still tender, and, when evening brings an end to his activities, he metes out the tribute due to the necessities of his stomach, and then sleeps the sweeter, enjoying a rest that none could grudge after his exertions during the day" (*Affairs of the Heart* 44-45).

Among the Jews, children grew from childhood to maturity by participating in the life of their family (cf. pp. 37-40) while schools came into being only in the 1st century B.C. (cf. pp. 40-42).

Boys were considered to be adults at thirteen and girls at twelve. From then onwards, they had to fulfil all the duties of an Israelite. A late addition in the *Mishnah* contains a saying which is attributed by some to Rabbi Samuel the Younger (end of 1st century A.D.). He divided life as follows:

"At five years old, (one is fit) for the Scripture; at ten years for the *Mishnah*; at thirteen for (the fulfilling of) the commandments; at fifteen for the *Talmud*; at eighteen for the bride chamber; at twenty for pursuing (a calling); at thirty for authority; at forty for discernment; at fifty for counsel; at sixty for to be an elder; at seventy for grey hairs; at eighty for special strength; at ninety for bowed back; and at a hundred a man is as one that has (already) died and passed away and ceased from the world" (*Aboth* 5.21).

Even before the age of five, children had to learn by participation in worship:

"As soon as a child is free from his mother's care, he is old enough to be under the obligation of dwelling in the Tabernacle, on the Feast of Tabernacles. If he knows how to wave the palm branch, he must wave one. If he understands the commandments of fringes and phylacteries and can put them on, it is his father's duty to provide him with them. As soon as he can speak, his father teaches him the *Shema*, *Torah* and the sacred tongue; otherwise, it were better he had not come into the world" (*Tosefta Hagigah* 1, 2).

It has already been shown that children were important essentially as schoolchildren (cf. the rabbinic sayings quoted on pp. 11, 42 ff.). This was accompanied by a tremendous respect for teachers. Just as the safety of a city was believed to depend upon the seriousness of the schoolchildren's learning, so it also depended upon their teachers' work. The *Jerusalem Talmud* reports that Rabbi Yuda Nesiah (early 3rd century A.D.) sent colleagues:

"to traverse the cities in the land of Israel in order to appoint Bible and *Mishnah* teachers. They came to a city, and they found no teacher of Bible or *Mishnah*. They said, 'Bring to us the guardians of the city.' So they brought to them the senators of the town. They said: 'Are these the guardians of the town? They are the destroyers of the town.' 'Who then', they said, 'are the guardians of the town?' They said: 'The teachers of Bible and *Mishnah*', as it is said, 'Unless the Lord guard the city, the watchman wakes but in vain' (Ps. 127: 1)" (*Hagigah* 1, §7, f, 76c).

The rabbis wondered who would sit at the right hand of God. One of them said:

"It is they who come before God because of their knowledge of the Law, and because of their good deeds. Another Rabbi said: It is the class of those teachers of Scripture and *Mishnah* who teach the children faithfully, for they will sit at God's right hand" (*Pesikta Kahana* 180a).

The religious significance of children

The rediscovery of the child in the Graeco-Roman world (cf. pp. 7 ff.) was partly due to the religious significance assigned to children. The expected saviour of the world was sometimes visualized in the form of a divine-human boy who would inaugurate the golden age (cf. the *Fourth Eclogue* of Virgil, p. 8 above).

Children are still unconscious of their sexuality. Therefore, they were considered to be sexually innocent, and as such could serve as religious mediums. The Roman poet, Catullus (1st century B.C.), described the children who served the goddess Diana with the following, freely translated verses:

> "We girls and boys who are still whole,
> under protection of Diana;
> We boys and girls who are still whole
> sing praises to Diana" (*Poems* 34, 1-4).

This same type of innocence of children appears in the apocryphal *Gospel of Thomas* (cf. p. 24). There, becoming like a child is equated with making "the male and the female into a single one" (*Logion* 22).

The goal of redemption is seen as a return to the childlike state before the fall. "Jesus said: 'From Adam to John the Baptist, there is none born of women who is higher than John the Baptist'... But I have said, He who shall be among you as a little one shall know the Kingdom, and shall be higher than John" (*Logion* 46).

Those who have become a new Adam in such a way have reached the original state of innocence. Therefore, the Jesus of the Gospel of Thomas says: "When you unclothe yourselves and are not ashamed, and take your garments and lay them beneath your feet like little children... then (shall ye see) the Son of the Living One, and ye shall not fear" (*Logion* 37).

Those who have been transformed into such innocence will be the truly wise. "Jesus said: 'The man aged in his days will not hesitate to ask a little child of seven days about the place of life, and he shall live. For there are many first who shall be last, and they shall become a single one' " (*Logion* 4).

The rabbinic sayings also contain a few affirmations about the innocence of children which give them a special relationship to God. However, the accent lies there less on sexual innocence and more on God's special love for those who are weak and need protection (cf. pp. 27 ff.). Thus, even the stammering of children delights God.

Rabbi Issachar (ca. 300 A.D.) "said of a child who says Masha for Moses, Ahran for Aaron, and for Ephron, Aphron, that God says: 'Even his stammering I love' (a pun on Cant. 2 : 4. 'His banner *(diglo)* over me is love'; for *diglo* the *Midrash* reads *dillugo*)... The rabbis say: A child may jump over the holy name of God again and again, and he is not punished; yea, even more, For God says, 'His very jumping I love' (*dillugo* for *diglo*)" (*Cant. Rabbah II*, §4, 1).

Rabbi Huna (ca. 300 A.D.) said: "Because twice daily, once in the morning and once in the evening, the children in the Synagogue say, 'Save us, O Lord our God' (Ps. 106 : 47), therefore God also says twice daily, 'O that the time would approach when I could cause your redemption to draw nigh' (cf. Ps. 14 : 7; 53 : 6)" (*Pesikta Rabbati* 174a).

In the saying of Rabbi Juda Nesiah quoted earlier, according to which "the world stands only upon the breath of the schoolchildren" (cf. p. 42), there is a significant addition which records the following discussion: "Rabbi Papa (4th century A.D.) said to Abbai: 'How about your breath and mine?' Abbai replied: 'The breath of them that are sinful cannot be compared with the breath of them that are not sinful' " (*Sabbath* 119b).

A child was thought to be without sin, not because it had as yet no evil *yetzer*, that is, no "evil inclination". For according to the rabbis, God himself said: "It was I who put the bad leaven in the dough, for the *yetzer* of the heart of man is evil from his youth" (*Tanhuma B., Noah* 15b). Yet some of the rabbis thought that little children had not yet given the evil inclination a chance to grow. "Why does a child of five, six, seven, eight or nine years not sin, but only at ten years and upwards? He himself makes his *yetzer* big. *You* make your *yetzer* bad" (*Tanhuma, Bereshit*, §7, f, 10a). This is the reason why older children must study the *Torah*. For Raba (4th century A.D.) said: "Though God created the evil *yetzer*, He created the Law, as an antidote against it" (*Baba Batra* 16a).

These reflections of the rabbis about the *yetzer* show why schoolchildren were considered to be so dear to God. At the same time, these reflections explain why infants could become the pledges for the covenant, as the following rabbinic story shows:

"When God was about to give the *Torah* to Israel, He asked them, 'Will you accept my *Torah*?' and they answered, 'We will.' God said: 'Give me surety that you will fulfil its ordinances.' They said: 'Let Abraham, Isaac and Jacob be our pledges.' God answered: 'But the patriarchs themselves need sureties. Did not Abraham show lack of faith (Gen. 15 : 8); Isaac, a love for my foe Esau (Mal. 1 : 3), Jacob, a want of belief in my protection (Isa. 40: 27)?' [Then Israel said: 'Let the prophets be our sureties.' But, 'the prophets have sinned against me' (Jer. 2 : 8)]. Then Israel said: 'Our children shall be our sureties.' [God said: 'Such pledges will I indeed accept.' Straightway the Israelites brought their wives with their children, even infants at the breast, even babes yet unborn. And God gave power of speech even to those yet in the womb. He said to them, 'I am about to give the *Torah* to your parents, will you pledge yourselves that they will fulfil it?' They said: 'We pledge ourselves.' Then God rehearsed command after command, and to each in succession the children promised obedience. How do we know that it was on the sucklings and babes yet unborn that the *Torah* was based?] As it says: 'Out of the mouths of babes and sucklings has strength been based' (Ps. 8 : 2), for the strength which God gives his people is *Torah* (Ps. 29 : 1). So it is that, when Israel neglects the *Torah*, God demands the penalty from the sureties, as it is said: 'Thou didst forget the *Torah* of thy God, I, also I, will forget thy children' (Hos. 4 : 7). Why 'also I'? God says: 'Also I am grieved for them, the children [to whom the parents have not taught *Torah*], who say daily: "Blessed be the Lord, who is to be blessed for evermore" ' " (*Tanhuma*, *Wayiggash*, §2, f, 67b; additions in square brackets from *Midrash 'Asereth ha-Dibroth*).

Appendix D · Study Outlines and Worksheets

If a Bible study group wants to work on the texts relating to Jesus and the children, it would be helpful for each study if every participant had a copy of the relevant *worksheet* in hand. Individual readers may also want to tear out and stick together these worksheets in order to have the texts arranged in the synoptic order beside the book while reading the corresponding chapters.

The suggested *study outlines* must, of course, be adapted for each particular group and occasion. The composition of the participants and their experience may make it imperative to start with other questions than those suggested. Moreover, the dynamics of group discussion will lead different groups into different directions. The study leader who guides the group's work will have to ensure that both the biblical text and the questions of the participants are being heard. The leader must, therefore, sometimes play the role of advocate for the text and sometimes that of advocate for minority voices in the group.

The study outlines all follow the same general pattern. Under the title "Introduction", a procedure and a question are suggested by which the members of the group are called upon to participate actively in the study process from the very beginning. The leader will have to make sure that this introductory period remains short and to the point. The main part of the time available should be devoted to the task(s) described under the title "Study of the Text", which usually involves small group work and general discussion. Some groups will not have enough time for the two tasks which are suggested in each outline. In this case, preferably the first task should be dealt with. Under the title "A Text for Today", each outline proposes a procedure, question or work assignment by which the Bible study can lead to prayer and be followed up by a process of actual "living with the text" in everyday life. It is essential that this third phase of work not be done hurriedly in the last 2-3 minutes, but that sufficient time be planned for it.

The study outlines were written for groups which can meet for periods of 1½-2 hours. At the risk of sounding too school-masterly, approximate spans of time are indicated for each step in the proposed process of study. Each group will, of course, develop its own pace, and the study leader must be sensitive to this, so that the work neither drags nor is done too hastily. One must in any case reckon with the fact that, however much time is available, there will always be more questions raised than answered.

The studies are planned in such a way, that they can be done by very small groups, by larger groups of 10-50 and by much larger assemblies. In such large gatherings, the study leader does not have to become a lecturer. Each participant can actively join in the learning process if enough time is given for personal reflection on the questions asked, and if the work on the tasks given is done in small buzz-groups with one's neighbours in the hall. In this case, the general discussion in large assemblies will have to be replaced by a public panel discussion between the study leader and two or three representative participants. In groups of up to 25, the best seating arrangement is obviously a circle with no second rows.

Before devoting four or more sessions to the study of the biblical texts dealt with in this book, groups would do well to devote two or more initial sessions to being informed about and discussing the following subjects: (1) What is the role of children in the life and education of our own society today? (2) What was the position of the child in the life and education of the Graeco-Roman and the Jewish world at the time of the New Testament? (For the latter subject, some of the Graeco-Roman and Jewish texts quoted in chapters 1 and 4 and Appendix C might be good discussion starters).

For the sessions devoted to the Bible studies, this book is intended only as background reading for the study leader and not as a study manual for the group itself. Similarly, the study outlines are merely suggestions for the leader which he or she should use in such a way that neither the group nor the leader becomes a slave to the outlines. Only the worksheets are needed by the participants.

Thus, the corporate exploration of the texts on Jesus and the children can lead the participants to new discoveries. And it is to be hoped that the fruit of this study will be a new quality of life together with the children in our families, local churches and neighbourhoods.

Study Outline I

Introduction

We all have seen children playing together.

Question: Which things strike you most as you remember such children playing?

After the participants have talked over this question with the person sitting beside them (about 5 minutes) some of these off-hand impressions about children playing are shared with the total group (5-10 minutes). The Bible study leader then recounts that Jesus also once observed a group of children playing and that this became for him a parable. At this point, copies of Worksheet I are handed out.

Study of the text

Question: Read Matt. 11 : 16-17 and Luke 7 : 31-35. Guess what the children wanted to play. How did this particular game end?

After a few minutes of silent study, some answers to the above question are discussed (this should not take longer than 5-10 minutes). The leader then introduces the first main task.

Task 1: Sometimes this parable has been explained in the following way. The first group of children represents Jesus who came with an invitation to the messianic feast. The second group of children represents John the Baptist who had come earlier with a call to conversion and repentance. Yet those who are called here "this generation" misunderstand and reject both John and Jesus. Does this explanation of the parable do justice to what is actually said in Matt. 11 : 16-19 and Luke 7 : 31-35? If not, what did Jesus want to communicate to the Jewish crowds and their leaders by this parable and its application?

For this task, the group is divided into sub-groups of 3-5 people. After about 15 minutes' sub-group discussion, various opinions about the above questions are brought before the total group. In this general discussion, the distinction between a parable and an allegory and the polemic function of this particular parable might have to be clarified. Also, the differing meanings of the children *(paidia)* in the parable and the "children of wisdom" *(tekna* in Luke 7 : 35) will probably have to be explained. The discussion will almost certainly raise the question about who is referred to by the expression "this generation". This will lead to a consideration of the context into which this parable has been placed, especially Matt. 11 : 4-5; Luke 7 : 22-23 and Luke 7 : 29-30. (For this task, that is, discussion in the sub-groups and the general discussion, some 30-40 minutes must be allowed.) If there is enough time, the leader then introduces the second main task.

(Continued on page 82.)

WORKSHEET I

We Piped, and You Did Not Dance

Matthew 11 : 16-19

16 "But to what shall I compare this generation?
It is like children sitting in the market places and calling to their playmates,
17 'We piped to you, and you did not dance; we wailed, and you did not mourn.'
18 For John came neither eating nor drinking and they say: 'He has a demon'; 19 the Son of man came eating and drinking, and they say: 'Behold, a glutton and a drunkard, a friend of tax collectors and sinners!' Yet wisdom is justified by her deeds."

Luke 7 : 31-35

31 "To what, then, shall I compare the men of this generation, and what are they like? 32 They are like children sitting in the market place and calling to one another,
'We piped to you, and you did not dance; we wailed, and you did not weep.'
33 For John the Baptist has come eating no bread and drinking no wine; and you say, 'He has a demon.' 34 The Son of man has come eating and drinking; and you say: 'Behold, a glutton and a drunkard, a friend of tax collectors and sinners!' 35 Yet wisdom is justified by all her children."

Context

Matthew 11	Luke 7
v. 2 "Now when John heard in prison about the deeds of the Christ…"	v. 18 "The disciples of John told him of all these things…"
vv. 2-6 John the Baptist's question and Jesus' answer.	vv. 18-23 John the Baptist's question and Jesus' answer. v. 21 Jesus performs healings while the emissaries are there.
vv. 7-19 Jesus' witness concerning John. v. 12 "the men of violence" vv. 13 ff. John = Elijah	vv. 24-35 Jesus' witness concerning John.
[cf. Matt. 21 : 31b-32]	[cf. Luke 16 : 16]
	v. 29 ff. "all the people and the tax collectors justi-fied God…"

Parable and application

Matthew 11	Luke 7
vv. 20-24 Woes pronounced on Galilean cities. [cf. Matt. 26 : 6-13; Mark 14 : 3-9 and John 12 : 1-8]	[cf. Luke 10 : 12-15]
	vv. 36-40 Jesus forgives the woman who sinned and who came to anoint his feet.
vv. 25-27 Jesus' thanksgiving to the Father.	[cf. Luke 10 : 21-22]

Task 2: Matthew and Luke give us slightly different versions of this parable and its application. Moreover, while both put it into the context of Jesus' witness concerning John the Baptist, they have edited this context differently. Compare Matthew's version and context with that of Luke and vice-versa. What is specific to each of the evangelists? What can we learn from this for the particular testimony of Matthew and the particular testimony of Luke?

For this task, the group can best be divided into two; one half examines Matthew's and the other Luke's version, context and testimony. If these two groups are too large, it would be best for them to work in smaller sub-groups. It is not necessary to have a general discussion for this task, and the two groups should be given 20-30 minutes for the synoptic comparison and the discovery of the two evangelists' main testimonies.

A text for today

Towards the end of the session, the leader gives a short summary of some of the insights gained by the group. He then introduces the final question with words such as these.

In the next sessions of our group, we will study other texts from the gospels which tell of what Jesus wants to teach us through children. The children, as Jesus sees them, will lead us to reconsider our priorities in life and to reverse much of our pedagogies. In the text which we studied today, the children function as a mirror for what is called here "this generation", that is, those Jews and their leaders who did not recognize that with John the Baptist and Jesus the decisive hour for their lives and for world history had come. Some of us may, of course, be a bit disappointed that, according to this first text which we studied, Jesus sees in the children's attitude a parable of unbelief. Yet this shows us that Jesus did not romantically idealize the children and that we should not do so either.

Today, too, children can be for us as a mirror where we discover our own unbelief. In these last moments of our study together, we therefore want to come back to today's children, those whom we know personally in our families and neighbourhoods.

Question: How do the children who we know personally mirror our own unbelief?

This question can simply be proposed to the participants as an assignment for homework and for their own self-examination. It may also lead to a last group discussion after some time of silent reflection. Or the question can introduce a moment of corporate prayer. After a period of silent meditation, some participants may want to share with the group spontaneous prayers of confession in relation to the question asked. Such confessions of unbelief can best be concluded by a word of forgiveness and assurance (for example, Matt. 11 : 28-30) and/or the prayer: "Lord, we believe, help our unbelief", said in unison.

Study Outline II

Introduction

We do not know what Jesus looked like. We have records of his words and deeds, of his life, death and resurrection, but we do not have any portrait of him, not even a description of his physical appearance. Nevertheless, most of us have an "image" of Jesus. Before turning to the text of today, we are going to share our different images of Jesus with one another.

Question: How do you imagine Jesus? Attempt to visualize him and describe what he looks like for you.

After a few minutes of silent "visualizing", the participants share their image of Jesus with those sitting beside them. Afterwards, some participants describe their image to the whole group. If all participants of a parish group know a painting, sculpture or stained-glass window of Jesus in their own church building, one might phrase the question differently, namely: You all know the representation of Jesus in our sanctuary. Is this the way in which you yourselves imagine Jesus or how else would you represent him? This introductory period should not take longer than a quarter of an hour.

Study of the text

Copies of Worksheet II are handed out and the leader briefly explains why the saying of Jesus in Mark 10 : 15 is left out of this particular study. (Cf. footnote on Worksheet II). Mark's version of the story (without v. 15) is then read.

Question: What is the image of Jesus which we receive through his words and actions in this story?

After a few off-the-cuff comments from participants, the first main task is introduced.

Task 1 (a): On the worksheet, you find a quotation from the Greek historian, Herodot, who describes what happened when children were born in Sparta. (Here the study leader or preferably another member of the group who was asked to come prepared for this task gives a 5-10 minute discourse on child-exposure in the ancient world). This text of Herodot and the text from Mark 10 : 13-16 reveal two totally different attitudes to children. Discover and describe these two different attitudes. Examine whether in our own society somewhat comparable differences of attitudes to children exist.

(Continued on page 86.)

WORKSHEET II

Let The Children Come To Me

Mark 10 : 13-16 [13] "And they were bringing children to him, that He might touch them; and the disciples rebuked them. [14] But when Jesus saw it, He was indignant, and said to them: 'Let the children come to me, do not hinder them; for to such belongs the Kingdom of God.' [15] . . . . * . . . [16] And He took them in his arms and blessed them, laying his hands upon them."

* For this study, v. 15 is left out for two reasons. (1) The saying on the receiving of the Kingdom will be the main text of study III. (2) At the stage of oral tradition, the context of this saying of Jesus was probably not yet fixed. Mark and Luke relate it to the scene where Jesus lets the children come to him (Mark 10 : 13-16; Luke 18 : 15-17, but it is missing in the parallel account of Matt. 19 : 13-15), while Matthew and John report a similar saying of Jesus in two other contexts (cf.: Matt. 18 : 1-5 and John 3 : 3-5).

Text for comparison

Plutarch on children in Sparta

"Offspring was not reared at the will of the father, but was taken and carried by him to a place called Lesche, where the elders of the tribes officially examined the infant, and if it was well-built and sturdy, they ordered the father to rear it, and assigned it one of the nine thousand lots of land; but if it was ill-born and deformed, they sent it to the so-called Apothetae, a chasm-like place at the foot of Mount Taÿgetus, in the conviction that the life of that which nature had not well equipped at the very beginning for health and strength, was of no advantage either to itself or the state" (*Lycurgus* 16, 1 ff.).

After individual study and exchange with neighbours or work in small groups, the discoveries are reported to the whole group and discussed. For this task (introduction, reflection, discussion), some 30-40 minutes must be allowed.

If the group has already spent a whole session on the position of children in the Graeco-Roman and Jewish world, instead of task 1 (a) the following task 1 (b) might be proposed which will take about the same amount of time.

Task 1 (b): Compare Mark 10 : 13-16 with two other incidents in the life of Jesus which are reported in Mark 8 : 29-35 and Mark 14 : 3-9. What do these two stories have in common with Mark 10 : 13-16? What can we learn from them for the understanding of Jesus' saying and actions in Mark 10 : 13-16? This task can best be done in small groups.

Task 2: Since the Middle Ages, this story has usually been read during children's baptismal services. Obviously, Mark 10 : 13-16 does not speak about baptism, just as the New Testament texts on baptism do not speak about children (except in the inclusive way when a whole family is baptized; cf. Acts 16 : 33). Which understanding of children's baptism underlines the basic message of Mark 10 : 13-16 and which understanding of children's baptism contradicts what Jesus wants to teach us through Mark 10 : 13-16?

Reflection on this subject can be done in small groups or in a general discussion (lasting about 30 minutes). It would be good if the participants were led by the study of Mark 10 : 13-16 to examine critically their own and their churches' understanding and practice of baptism.

A text for today
The story which we studied does not so much tell us something about the character of children, but about the character of God.

Question: In the Apostles' Creed, we confess: "I believe in God the Father Almighty, Maker of heaven and earth." How could we express in a similar short confessional sentence the God who meets us in Mark 10 : 13-16?

Each participant is asked to write down on paper a one-sentence confession of this kind. Some of these are then read aloud. The best ones (that is, those which confess most clearly the central message of Mark 10 : 13-16) are retained and each participant chooses one of these to write down.

Assignment: Each participant will attempt to live daily with the adopted confessional statement until the next meeting of the group. Write the statement on a small card, carry it always with you, learn it by heart and repeat it several times a day while remembering the story of Mark 10 : 13-16. Attempt to live your relationships within the family, with neighbours and colleagues according to this confession and let this confession become operative in your decisions. We will start our next group session by telling one another how this confession functioned in our daily life.

Study Outline III

Introduction

From the story of Jesus who lets the children come to him we learned more about the nature of God than about the nature of children. He is a God who graciously gives his Kingdom to children. On the basis of our study we formulated a short confessional statement, and promised to one another to live with this confession in our everyday life.

Question: How has this confession influenced your thinking, attitudes and decisions over the last week(s)?

After neighbours have exchanged views, some positive or negative experiences are brought before the total group. Of course, many people may have become aware of how little impact our statements of faith have on our actual life, and this disturbing discovery may become the main topic of discussion (10-20 minutes for this introductory phase).

If at the end of the second session the group has not committed itself to do the above-described homework, this third study can immediately begin with the following question concerning different uses of language.

Study of the text

There are many different uses of language. If one is not sensitive to this fact, serious misunderstandings can arise.

Question: What is the difference in the use of language if you say to somebody: "this is a stone", or "your head is a stone"?

A short discussion will highlight the differences between descriptive and evocative language. At this point, the term "metaphor" is introduced and explained. Copies of Worksheet III are handed out and the attention of the participants is drawn to the fact that, in Mark 10 : 15 and parallels, Jesus uses metaphorical language.

Task 1: Compare the five different versions of the saying of Jesus in Mark 10 : 15; Luke 18 : 17; Matt. 18 : 3; John 3 : 3-5 and the Logion 22 of the Gospel of Thomas. What are the similarities and differences in the wording and the context of this saying? Are there any substantial differences of meaning in these different versions?

For this task the group can best be divided into 5 sub-groups. Each of these is assigned one of the five versions for comparison with the other four and for discovering the particular message of their version. Small group work and general discussion on this task will take some 35-45 minutes.

(Continued on page 90.)

WORKSHEET III

Unless You Become Like a Child

Matthew 18 : 3

Jesus "said: 'Truly, I say to you, unless you turn and become like children, you will never enter the Kingdom of Heaven'."

Context: Part of the scene where Jesus teaches about true greatness, at the beginning of the discourse on the Church (Matt. 18).

Mark 10 : 15

"Truly, I say to you, whoever does not receive the Kingdom of God like a child shall not enter it."

Context: Part of the scene where Jesus lets the children come to him, within the catechetical instruction on marriage, children and wealth (Mark 10 : 1-22).

Luke 18 : 17

"Truly, I say to you, whoever does not receive the Kingdom of God like a child shall not enter it."

Context: Part of the scene where Jesus lets the children come to him, following the parables of the unjust judge and the Pharisee and tax collector (Luke 18 : 1-14).

Gospel of Thomas, Logion 22

"Jesus saw some infants at the breast. He said to his disciples: 'These little ones are like those who enter the Kingdom.' They said to him: 'If we then be children, shall we enter the Kingdom?' Jesus said to them: ... 'When you make the male and the female into a single one..., then you shall enter (the Kingdom).'"

Context: One of the unrelated 114 sayings of Jesus in the apocryphal Gospel of Thomas from the 2nd century A.D.

John 3 : 3-5

"Jesus answered him: 'Truly, truly, I say to you, unless one is born anew * , he cannot see the Kingdom of God.' Nicodemus said to him: 'How can a man be born when he is old? Can he enter a second time into his mother's womb and be born?' Jesus answered: 'Truly, truly, I say to you, unless one is born of water and the Spirit, he cannot enter the Kingdom of God!'"

Context: The conversation with the Pharisee Nicodemus.

---

* The original Greek can also be translated with "born from above" instead of "born anew".

Rabbinic texts

Several sayings of Jewish rabbis relate the receiving of the Kingdom with the recital of the *Shema*, which is the basic Jewish prayer and watchword combining Deuteronomy 6 : 4-9 with Deuteronomy 11 : 13-21 and later also Numbers 15 : 37-47. The *Shema* must be prayed twice a day by every believing Jew. The rabbis quoted lived in the 2nd and 3rd centuries A.D., but they may have preserved an oral tradition going back to pre-Christian times.

Deuteronomy Rabbah: "Rabbi Judah said in the name of Rab: 'He who has to say the *Shema* while he is out walking must stand still, and receive the Kingdom of Heaven. And what is the Kingdom of Heaven? The Lord our God, the Lord is One'" (2, 31).

Tanhuma, Lekleka: "How is a wayfarer to pray? He must not take the Kingdom of Heaven upon himself while he is walking, but he must pause, direct his heart to God with awe and fear, trembling and quaking, at the proclamation of the divine unity, as he utters the *Shema*, every single word with heartfelt sincerity, and then he should recite the doxology. But when he begins the following paragraph, he may, if he so desires, resume his journey and pray as he walks..." (§1, f, 24a).

Tosefta Hagigah: "As soon as he (a boy) can speak, his father teaches him the *Shema*, *Torah* and the sacred tongue; otherwise, it were better he had not come into the world" (1,2).

During the general discussion, the text from the Gospel of Thomas particularly will need some explanation from the study leader. It may also be necessary during the discussion to comment on the biblical meaning of "humbleness", i.e. not in the first place a subjective state of mind but an objective state of dependency.

Task 2: The expression "to receive the Kingdom of God" (Mark 10 : 15; Luke 18 : 17) occurs only here in the New Testament. Yet there are rabbinic sayings which use this expression in connection with the daily recital of the *Shema* (see Worksheet III). What light do these rabbinic sayings throw on both the common and the different ways in which Jews and Christians see a life that leads to the "receiving of the Kingdom"?

Some 20-30 minutes should be allowed for considering this question. However, if participants have had no introductory session on the child in the Jewish world and have never seen rabbinic texts, either more time must be allowed for information about rabbinic Judaism or this second task must be dropped.

A text for today
   "Like a child" is a metaphor for a total attitude in our relationships with fellow human beings and with God. Like every metaphor, it evokes different things in different people, and we must therefore let our partial understandings be corrected and complemented by the biblical text and by one another's insights.

   Question: What does it mean today to be "like a child" in the everyday life of our society? What, today, is the opposite to being "like a child"?

In order to sharpen our eyes ready for modern parables and/or visual metaphors of what it means to be "like a child", the following assignment for homework can be given. Read the daily newspaper and look at illustrated magazines with a view to finding some striking contemporary examples of being or not being "like a child". Group members should be asked to bring relevant newspaper and magazine clippings to the next session. Such clippings can then be tacked on to the notice-board and thus be shared with other group members.

If time allows (that is, if at least 30 minutes are left), it is much better to begin this exercise of discernment, as a group, during the closing period of the session. In this case, small sub-groups are given a copy of a daily newspaper or an illustrated magazine. On the basis of modern parables and metaphors of being "like a child" which they have discovered, each sub-group prepares a short prayer of confession of sin, intercession or thanksgiving. The session ends with a moment of worship consisting of these prayers.

Study Outline IV

Introduction

If study III ended as was suggested, and the participants have found in newspapers and magazines some striking examples of what it means today to be "like a child", then the session can begin with an informal sharing of such modern parables and visual metaphors. Then copies of Worksheet IV are distributed and the session begins with a short discussion of Plato's definition of education as printed on the worksheet.

Question: What is the aim of education according to Plato? Do you agree with it?

Study of the text

After some 15 minutes general discussion on educational aims and practices, the study leader introduces the biblical text. In answer to the question: "Who is the greatest?", Jesus put a child in the midst of his disciples; a child, not to be taught, but as a model for teaching the disciples. A child, not as the "raw material for education", but as the desired end result of true greatness and education. An actual child was involved in the incident. According to the reporting of the evangelists, however, a shift occurs from descriptive to metaphorical language. The "child" becomes a metaphor for the Church, but the nuances vary according to the evangelist who is writing.

Task 1: Compare the three parallel accounts of the teaching on true greatness. Notice similarities, differences and the particularities of each evangelist. Then read for each the additional passages indicated. Who is symbolized by the "child" in Matthew's, Mark's and Luke's testimonies?

The group is divided into three: a sub-group for Matthew, one for Mark and one for Luke. After these sub-groups have worked for 20-30 minutes, they report their findings to one another.

The study leader then introduces the second task. Should there not be enough time to deal with both tasks, the second should be given priority.

Task 2: "Whoever receives this child in my name receives me, and whoever receives me receives him who sent me". For Jesus, the child represents himself and therefore God. Compare this saying with the rabbinic saying on the worksheet about teachers. What does this comparison show us about similarities and differences between the pedagogy of the rabbis and the pedagogy of Jesus?

(Continued on page 94.)

WORKSHEET IV

A Child in the Midst of Them

Matthew 18 : 1-5	*Mark 9 : 33-37*	*Luke 9 : 46-48*
	33 And they came to Capernaum; and when He was in the house He asked them: "What were you discussing on the way?" 34 But they were silent; for on the way they had discussed with one another who was the greatest.	46 And an argument arose among them as to which of them was the greatest.
1 At that time, the disciples came to Jesus, saying: "Who is the greatest in the Kingdom of Heaven?"	35 And He sat down and called the twelve; and He said to them: "If any one would be first, he must be last of all and servant of all."	
2 And calling to him a child, He put him in the midst of them, 3 and said	36 And He took a child, and put him in the midst of them; and taking him in his arms, He said to them:	47 But when Jesus perceived the thought of their hearts, He took a child and put him by his side, 48 and said to them,
"Truly, I say to you, unless you turn and become like children, you will never enter the Kingdom of Heaven. 4 Whoever humbles himself like this child, he is the greatest in the Kingdom of Heaven.		
5 Whoever receives one such child in my name receives me."	37 "Whoever receives one such child in my name receives me; and whoever receives me, receives not me, but him who sent me."	"Whoever receives this child in my name receives me, and whoever receives me receives him who sent me; for he who is least among you all is the one who is great."

Texts for Comparison

Plato on education: "The education we speak of is training from childhood in goodness, which makes a man eagerly desirous of becoming a perfect citizen, understanding how both to rule and to be ruled righteously... An upbringing which aims only at money making, or physical strength, or even some mental accomplishment devoid of reason and justice, it would term vulgar and illiberal and utterly unworthy of the name 'education'." (*Laws* 644a).

Child as metaphor: For Matthew: cf. Matt. 18:5-6, 10-14; 10:40-42.
For Mark: cf. Mark 9:41-42.
For Luke: cf. Luke 12:22-32, especially verse 32.

Rabbinic sayings on teachers

"The one who receives the scribes is like one who receives the *Shechinah*" (*Berakhoth* 64a; the *Shechinah* means God's own presence in the form of light and glory).

"The rabbis wondered who would sit at the right hand of God. One of them said: 'It is they who come before God because of their knowledge of the Law, and because of their good deeds.' Another rabbi said: 'It is the class of those teachers of Scripture and *Mishnah* who teach the children faithfully, for they will sit at God's right hand' (*Pesikta Kahana* 180a)."

In this discussion, it will probably be necessary to feed in additional information about education in the Old Testament and rabbinic times. At least 30 minutes should be allowed for this task.

A text for today

Each group will have to find its own way concerning how to close this last study, and therefore will have to define itself the whole study process. The dignity of children as Jesus' and God's representatives in our midst will have to be emphasized. This should not remain on a general level, but concentrate on concrete implications of this dignity in fields where the participants can get actively involved.

If there are many parents and teachers among the participants, the group may want to continue the discussion on education. What are the implications of the dignity of children for the educational goals and practices in families and schools? How can these implications be put into practice?

If the participants are mainly people responsible for Sunday School and other church activities, the implications of the dignity of children for the whole of the Church's life and worship should be examined.

If the group consists of lay people involved in local politics, neighbourhood associations, etc., the implications of the dignity of children for the ordering of life in society should be explored.

By far the best way to deal with the matter of implications and active involvement would be to plan a final session at the end of Study IV. Thus, there would be sufficient time for the above-mentioned reflection, with a view to action, and the group could prepare together a service of commitment. After that, the group should stop meeting. Eternal study groups get stale! The only meaningful additional meeting would be a feast together with children.